Instant Pot Cookbook for Vegetarian

150 Delicious and Easy to Cook Vegetarian Recipes

for Your Instant Pot Electric Pressure Cooker

By Darlene V. Vanhoose

Table of Content

Nutritional Vegetables Recipes..39

Flavorful Rice, Beans and Lentils Recipes

Tasty Snacks Recipes

Hot and Cold Beverages Recipes

Introduction

With the rise in health issues and growing prices of meat, vegetarian diets are gaining popularity. A lot of people are switching towards vegetarian diets and there are many reasons for it. Here is a brief introduction to vegetarianism. The followers of vegetarianism are called vegetarians. They can be defined as individuals who don't consume any food which has been either directly or indirectly produced by a living or a dead animal or from aiding products in their production.

History of Vegetarianism

Though it is written in history books that vegetarianism appeared around the 19th century, it has taken much popularity in present times.

Throughout the course of history, many civilizations like Greek, Hindu & even Christianity have regarded it. Previously it was followed mainly either for religious reasons or philosophical reasons. But today, it is famous for its ethnicity, taste, health benefits and ecological reasons. There are various types of vegetarian diets and the degree of restrictions varies from one type to the other.

The most widely adopted is lacto-ovo vegetarianism. It excludes consuming meat, but allows consuming other animal related products like eggs & dairy products. It is the most common vegetarian diet. In addition to this, there is:
- *A diet exclusive of all animal related products except dairy products called a lacto vegetarian diet.*

- A diet exclusive of all animal related products except eggs called an ovo vegetarian diet.
- A diet which excludes all kinds of meat except fish called a pescetarian diet.
- A diet excluding all kinds of animal and animal derived products, called a vegan diet.

Nutritional particularities

Most vegetarians adopt lacto vegetarianism. It is particularly more famous because of it can provide a balance diet inclusive of all necessary food groups.

Deficiencies caused due to not consuming meat and fish can be prevented with the proper intake of eggs and other dairy related products.

- In context of micronutrients, iron is provided by cereals, eggs and pulses; Calcium is provided by dairy products; Vitamin B is provided by cereals (whole grains in particular); Vitamin A is provided by vegetables and fruits; Vitamin D is provided by dairy products and eggs.

- In order to be a healthy vegetarian, all these factors should be taken into account and get a balanced diet comprising of different foods (given below). The reason for a vegetarian diet being the most healthy is that you consume less cholesterol and saturated fat than any normal diet without compromising on the intake of other necessary nutrients.

- A more restrictive type of veganism has a potentially higher risk of deficiencies in proteins, zinc, iron, Vitamins A & D and necessary amino acids.

This can be overcome if you ever opt for becoming a vegan; research is the key point in remaining healthy and vegan throughout.

Ideal Daily Diet for Vegetarians:

Breakfast

- Dairy products like milk etc.
- Cereals or whole grains
- Fruits

Lunch

- Cereals/Grains & Pulses
- Eggs
- Any Salad
- Dairy Products

Dinner

- Grains/Cereals & vegetables
- Fruits
- Dairy Products like milk etc.
- Bread

Steps to Achieve Recommended Dietary Allowance:

- Consume 3-4 helpings of milk/eggs daily (if you don't have cholesterol problems) or add protein rich seeds and nuts to your meals like pumpkin etc.
- Consume at-least one grain/cereal based meal added with beans, soya or peas.

- Other than this you should consume vegetables, fruits, bread and oil-producing seeds like almonds etc.

What is Instant Pot?

With the advancement of technology in almost every field, culinary and kitchen related appliances have also been gaining technical advancements from time to time. One such innovative appliance is the Instant Pot. It is a much more developed shape of what you may call a pressure cooker or a sauté pan. Its appealing functions like making meals without effecting its taste and nutrients is what makes it highly reliable

Why is Instant Pot?

In a world where cooked meals pose much of an easy thing to do instead of cooking yourself some delicious food, instant pot is going to serve you with instant and healthy cooked food. The hasty routine of every individual has made his access to healthy food daily life has deprived almost every individual the access to healthy food rare and has caused severe impacts on their mental and physical problems.

With so much awareness campaigns being done these days regarding health issues and consuming a healthy diet, instant pot has turned out to be the solution of every person who wishes to have a healthy and balanced diet.
It is a technologically advanced, programmable pressure cooker having the function of Bluetooth connectivity with any Smart phone or tablet etc. this makes it much easier and convenient to use for the user. Above all, it cooks 2-

6 times faster than any other cooking utensil, making it more appealing. It is a single pot appliance and it keeps the food full of nutrients without altering its taste.

For all these reasons, instant pot has almost one million users on Amazon and has got amazing reviews from the consumers. Culinary has been revolutionized with its advent and the world is unable to resist it.

So, if your busy routine is not allowing you in having a healthy and balanced diet but you want to have a healthy lifestyle. An instant pot is going to provide you with a healthy, nutritional and yummy in taste food in short time. It is going to be a turning point in making you achieve a balanced healthy life style.

The Benefits of Instant Pot

But, being a 7-in-1 appliance is not the only benefit that the revolutionary Instant Pot provides with. There are a number of reasons why you should switch to pressure cooking with the instant pot:

It's Time Efficient-If you are a busy worker (and who isn't nowadays) then your time is most likely pretty limited. The instant pot can provide you with the chance to start home cooking again because it actually cooks the meals 70 percent faster than other appliances.

It Saves Money-The main benefit of the Instant Pot is the fact that it saves energy. Cooking 70 percent faster means using 70 percent less energy than other appliances, which cuts your electric bill significantly. Another way in which the Instant Pot can save you money is that it turns even the cheapest cuts of meats into restaurant-like incredible dishes.

Nutrient Preserving- Thanks to the pressure flow that circles inside the pot, the meals are cooked even, and all of the nutrients are preserved.

No Harmful Substances- Pressure cooking means cooking at a temperature that is higher than the point of boiling water. That being said, all of the harmful substances found on the food are lost during the process of cooking.

It is Convenient- Cooking has really never been easier. You ca simply dump your ingredients in the pot, close the lid, set the cooking mode and time, and you will get delicious results minutes later.

Tips for Instant Pot Users

➢ Always note the total cooking time.

➢ There is no need of a stove for an instant pot.

➢ Fill the pot with 1 cup of any liquid before cooking anything.

➢ Uncooked meal can be given extra time for coking.

➢ Its highly recommended to manually read the instant pot

➢ Be wiser in opting for a recipe. Go from easy to hard slowly.

➢ The pot should be clean and tidy.

➢ The pot shouldn't be filled more than 2/3 of its size.

Delicious Vegetarian Soup Recipes

1. Tomato Soup

Yield: 4 Servings

Total Time: 25 Minutes

Prep Time: 10 Minutes

Cook Time: 20 Minutes

Ingredients

- 3 pounds fresh tomatoes, chopped
- 2 teaspoons dried parsley, crushed
- 2 tablespoons homemade tomato sauce
- 4 cups low-sodium vegetable broth
- Freshly ground black pepper, to taste
- ¼ cup fresh basil, chopped
- 1 tablespoon olive oil
- 1 garlic clove, minced
- 2 tablespoons sugar
- 1 medium onion, chopped
- 2 teaspoons dried basil, crushed
- 1 tablespoon balsamic vinegar

Directions

1. Put the oil, garlic and onion in the Instant Pot and select "Sauté".

2. Sauté for 4 minutes and add the tomatoes, herbs, tomato sauce, broth and black pepper.

3. Cook for about 3 minutes and lock the lid.

4. Set the Instant Pot to "Soup" and cook for 10 minutes at high pressure.

5. Release the pressure quickly and stir in the vinegar and sugar.

6. Put the mixture in the immersion blender and puree the soup.

7. Garnish with basil and serve.

Nutritional Information per Serving:

Calories: 146; Total Fat: 4.5 g; Carbs: 23.5 g; Sugars: 16.4 g; Protein: 5.4 g; Cholesterol: 0 mg; Sodium: 110mg

2.Corn Soup

Yield: 4 Servings

Total Time: 15 Minutes

Prep Time: 10 Minutes

Cook Time: 5 Minutes

Ingredients

- 2 tablespoons butter
- 2 medium garlic cloves, thinly sliced
- 2 bay leaves
- 3 cups chicken stock
- 2 medium leeks, finely chopped
- 6 corn with cobs, cut in halves
- 4 sprigs Tarragon

- 1 tablespoon chives, minced
- Salt and black pepper, to taste

Directions:

1. Put the butter, garlic and leeks in the Instant Pot and select "Sauté".
2. Sauté for 4 minutes and add the bay leaves, corn with cobs, chicken stock and tarragon sprigs.
3. Set the Instant Pot to "Soup" and cook for 10 minutes at high pressure.
4. Release the pressure quickly and discard corn cobs, bay leaf and tarragon sprigs.
5. Transfer the mixture into the blender and puree the soup.
6. Season the corn soup with salt and pepper and simmer for 3 minutes.

Nutritional Information per Serving:

Calories: 323; Total Fat: 11.5g; Carbs: 55.8g; Sugars: 2.38g; Protein: 8.3g; Cholesterol: 24mg; Sodium: 667mg

3.Bacon Potato Cheesy Soup

Yield: 6 Servings

Total Time: 30 Minutes

Prep Time: 10 Minutes

Cook Time: 20 Minutes

Ingredients

- 8 large potatoes, peeled and cubed
- 1 teaspoon salt
- 2 cups half and half cream

- 1 teaspoon black pepper
- 2 tablespoons dried parsley
- 1 cup cheddar cheese, shredded
- 1 cup frozen corn
- 3 tablespoons butter
- ¼ teaspoon red paprika flakes
- 3 oz. cream cheese, cubed
- 6 slices meatless bacon, crumbled
- ½ cup onions, chopped
- 3 cups chicken broth

Directions:

1. Put the butter and onions in the Instant Pot and select "Sauté".
2. Sauté for 4 minutes and add salt, black pepper, paprika flakes, chicken broth, dried parsley and pepper.
3. Sauté for 4 minutes and half and half cream, cheddar cheese, frozen corn, cream cheese and bacon.
4. Place the trivet in the Instant Pot and put potatoes on it.
5. Set the Instant Pot to "Soup" and cook for 12 minutes at high pressure.
6. Release the pressure quickly and dish out the potatoes.
7. Mash the potatoes and put them back in the pot.

Nutritional Information per Serving:

Calories: 669; Total Fat: 28g; Carbs: 88g; Sugars: 7.5g; Protein: 20g; Cholesterol: 81mg; Sodium: 1041mg

4.Corn and Potato Soup

Yield: 4 Servings

Total Time: 27 Minutes

Prep Time: 10 Minutes

Cook Time: 17 Minutes

Ingredients

- 2 cups fresh corn kernels
- 2 large russet potatoes, peeled and chopped
- 2 tablespoons butter
- 2 celery stalks, chopped
- 2 garlic cloves, chopped finely
- 1 teaspoon black pepper, freshly ground
- 6 cups low-sodium vegetable broth
- 3 tablespoons corn-starch
- ¼ cup half-and-half
- 3 carrots, peeled and chopped
- 1 medium onion, chopped
- 2 tablespoons dried parsley, crushed

Directions:

1. Put the butter, carrot, celery, garlic and onions in the Instant Pot and select "Sauté".
2. Sauté for 4 minutes and add corn kernels, potatoes, broth, parsley and black pepper.
3. Set the Instant Pot to "Soup" and cook for 10 minutes at high pressure.
4. Release the pressure quickly and open the lid.

5. Dissolve the cornstarch in half-and-half and add to the Instant Pot.
6. Select "Sauté" and cook for about 3 minutes.

Nutritional Information per Serving:

Calories: 343; Total Fat: 8.7g; Carbs: 59.1g; Sugars: 8.2g; Protein: 10g; Cholesterol: 21mg; Sodium: 216mg

5.Creamy Broccoli Soup

Yield: 3 Servings

Total Time: 22 Minutes

Prep Time: 5 Minutes

Cook Time: 17 Minutes

Ingredients

- 1 cup broccoli florets, washed and blanched
- 2 garlic cloves, minced
- 2tablespoons butter
- 1 teaspoon black pepper, freshly ground
- ½ cup full fat milk
- 1 small onion, chopped
- 1 tablespoon celery leaves, chopped
- 1 teaspoon salt
- ½ cup cream
- 1 cup vegetable stock

Directions:

1. Put the butter, celery, garlic and onions in the Instant Pot and select "Sauté".
2. Sauté for 4 minutes and add broccoli florets, vegetable stock, salt and black pepper.
3. Set the Instant Pot to "Soup" and cook for 10 minutes at high pressure.
4. Release the pressure quickly and open the lid.
5. Put the mixture in the blender and add milk and cream.
6. Put back in the Instant Pot and let it simmer for 3 minutes.

Nutritional Information per Serving:

Calories: 134; Total Fat: 10.1g; Carbs: 8.9g; Sugars: 4.6g; Protein: 3.4g; Cholesterol: 29mg; Sodium: 894mg

6. Creamy Mushroom Soup

Yield: 4 Servings

Total Time: 25 Minutes

Prep Time: 10 Minutes

Cook Time: 15 Minutes

Ingredients

- 10 oz. cremini mushrooms, thinly sliced
- 1 tablespoon olive oil
- 3 garlic cloves, minced
- 2 carrots, peeled and diced
- ½ teaspoon dried thyme
- 4 cups chicken stock

- ½ cup half-and-half
- 2 tablespoons fresh parsley leaves, chopped
- 2 tablespoons butter
- 1 onion, diced
- 2 stalks celery, diced
- ¼ cup all-purpose flour
- 1 bay leaf
- 1 sprig rosemary

Directions:

1. Put the olive oil, mushrooms, carrot, butter, celery, garlic, thyme and onions in the Instant Pot and select "Sauté".
2. Sauté for 4 minutes and add in the flour until light brown.
3. Add bay leaf and chicken stock and close the lid.
4. Set the Instant Pot to "Soup" and cook for 10 minutes at high pressure.
5. Release the pressure quickly and add half and half.
6. Season with salt and black pepper and garnish with rosemary and parsley.

Nutritional Information per Serving:

Calories: 208; Total Fat: 13.6g; Carbs: 18g; Sugars: 4.8g; Protein: 5.1g; Cholesterol: 26mg; Sodium: 852mg

7.Pumpkin and Tomato Soup

Yield: 4 Servings

Total Time: 15 Minutes

Prep Time: 10 Minutes

Cook Time: 5 Minutes

Ingredients

- 4 tablespoons pumpkin puree
- 1 cup tomatoes, chopped
- 4 tablespoons butter
- 1 carrot, roughly chopped
- 1 potato, roughly diced
- 3 tablespoons sun dried tomatoes
- 4 cups water
- 1 onion, roughly sliced
- 3 tablespoons tomato paste
- 1 teaspoon pumpkin spice powder
- 2 teaspoons salt
- 2 pinches black pepper

Directions:

1. Put the butter, carrots and onions in the Instant Pot and select "Sauté".
2. Sauté for 4 minutes and add potatoes, tomatoes, tomato paste, sun dried tomatoes, pumpkin puree, water, salt and black pepper.
3. Set the Instant Pot to "Soup" and cook for 15 minutes at high pressure.
4. Release the pressure naturally and add blend the mixture to a smooth consistency.

5. Sprinkle pumpkin spice powder and serve.

Nutritional Information per Serving:

Calories: 190; Total Fat: 12.7g; Carbs: 18.5g; Sugars: 5.9g; Protein: 2.8g; Cholesterol: 31mg; Sodium: 1296mg

8.Bacon and Cauliflower Soup

Yield: 4 Servings

Total Time: 30 Minutes

Prep Time: 10 Minutes

Cook Time: 20 Minutes

Ingredients

- 3 cups cauliflower florets
- 12 slices of meatless bacon, crisp fried
- 2 tablespoons butter
- 4 cups chicken stock
- 1 large onion, chopped
- 4 potatoes, chopped
- ½ cup heavy cream
- 1 tablespoon salt
- 1 tablespoon black pepper

Directions:

1. Put the butter and onions in the Instant Pot and select "Sauté".
2. Sauté for 4 minutes and add potatoes, browned bacon, chicken stock and cauliflower florets.

3. Set the Instant Pot to "Soup" and cook for 15 minutes at high pressure.
4. Release the pressure naturally and blend all the ingredients to a smooth paste.
5. Season with salt and black pepper and add heavy cream.

Nutritional Information per Serving:

Calories: 344; Total Fat: 16.7g; Carbs: 44.1g; Sugars: 6.6g; Protein: 8.3g; Cholesterol: 36mg; Sodium: 2812mg

9.Spinach Cream Soup

Yield: 3 Servings

Total Time: 20 Minutes

Prep Time: 5 Minutes

Cook Time: 15 Minutes

Ingredients

- 1 cup spinach puree
- ½ cup fresh cream
- 3tablespoons butter
- 1 cup white sauce
- 3 garlic cloves, minced
- 1 medium onion, roughly sliced
- 1 tablespoon tomato paste
- 1 tablespoon sun dried tomatoes
- 4 cups water
- 2 teaspoons salt

- 2 pinches black pepper

Directions:

1. Put the butter, garlic, salt, black pepper and onions in the Instant Pot and select "Sauté".
2. Sauté for 4 minutes and add water, spinach puree and tomato paste.
3. Set the Instant Pot to "Soup" and cook for 10 minutes at high pressure.
4. Release the pressure naturally and add fresh cream and white sauce.
5. Blend the contents of the Instant Pot to a smooth consistency and garnish with sun dried tomatoes.

Nutritional Information per Serving:

Calories: 305; Total Fat: 23.7g; Carbs: 17.6g; Sugars: 6.7g; Protein: 5.9g; Cholesterol: 44mg; Sodium: 2103mg

10.Cheesy Red Beans Soup

Yield: 3 Servings

Total Time: 23 Minutes

Prep Time: 8 Minutes

Cook Time: 15 Minutes

Ingredients

- 1 cup red beans
- 3tablespoons butter
- 1 carrot, roughly chopped
- 1 medium onion, roughly sliced
- 3 garlic cloves, minced

- 3 tablespoons tomato paste
- ½ cup Mexican cheese, shredded
- ½ cup half and half
- 4 cups water
- 2 teaspoons salt
- 2 pinches black pepper
- Crunchy tortilla chips, to garnish

Directions:

1. Put the butter, garlic, salt, black pepper, carrots and onions in the Instant Pot and select "Sauté".
2. Sauté for 5 minutes and add red beans, water, tomato paste and salt.
3. Set the Instant Pot to "Soup" and cook for 8 minutes at high pressure.
4. Release the pressure naturally and add Mexican cheese and half and half.
5. Garnish with crispy tortilla chips and serve.

Nutritional Information per Serving:

Calories: 418; Total Fat: 18.5g; Carbs: 49g; Sugars: 5.9g; Protein: 17.6g; Cholesterol: 50mg; Sodium: 1729mg

11.Sour Cream Black Beans Soup

Yield: 3 Servings

Total Time: 20 Minutes

Prep Time: 7 Minutes

Cook Time: 13 Minutes

Ingredients

- 1 cup black beans
- 5 garlic cloves, minced
- 3 tablespoons tomato paste
- ¼ cup sour cream
- 4 cups water
- 3 tablespoons butter
- 1 onion, roughly sliced
- 1 potato, roughly diced
- 1 tablespoon sun dried tomatoes
- 2 tablespoons fresh cream
- 2 teaspoons salt
- 2 pinches black pepper
- Crunchy nachos chips, for garnish

Directions:

1. Put the butter, garlic and onions in the Instant Pot and select "Sauté".
2. Sauté for 3 minutes and add black beans, tomato paste, water, sun dried tomatoes, salt and black pepper.
3. Set the Instant Pot to "Soup" and cook for 10 minutes at high pressure.
4. Release the pressure naturally and add sour cream.
5. Blend the contents of the Instant Pot to a smooth consistency and serve with fresh cream and broken nachos chips.

Nutritional Information per Serving:

Calories: 339; Total Fat: 13.1g; Carbs: 45g; Sugars: 4.2g; Protein: 13.1g; Cholesterol: 30mg; Sodium: 1264mg

12.Basil Tomato Soup

Yield: 2 Servings

Total Time: 17 Minutes

Prep Time: 5 Minutes

Cook Time: 12 Minutes

Ingredients

- ½ cup tomatoes
- 2 tablespoons tomato paste
- 2 tablespoons sun dried tomatoes
- 2tablespoons butter
- 1tablespoon basil leaves, freshly chopped
- 1 carrot, roughly chopped
- 1 onion, roughly sliced
- 1 potato, roughly diced
- 4 cups water
- 2 teaspoons salt
- ¼ teaspoon black pepper

Directions:

1. Put the butter, onions, carrots, basil leaves, salt and black pepper in the Instant Pot and select "Sauté".

2. Sauté for 4 minutes and add potatoes,tomatoes, sun dried tomatoes, tomato paste and water.

3. Set the Instant Pot to "Soup" and cook for 8 minutes at high pressure.

4. Release the pressure naturally and blend the contents of the Instant Pot to a smooth consistency.

Nutritional Information per Serving:
Calories: 239; Total Fat: 12.8g; Carbs: 29.6g; Sugars: 7.6g; Protein: 4.2g;

Cholesterol: 31mg; Sodium: 2486mg

13.Feta Cheese and Spinach Soup

Yield: 3 Servings

Total Time: 25 Minutes

Prep Time: 10 Minutes

Cook Time: 15 Minutes

Ingredients

- 1 cup spinach puree
- ½ cup feta cheese, crumbled
- 3tablespoons butter
- 4garlic cloves, minced
- 1 onion, roughly sliced
- 1 tablespoon tomato paste
- 1 tablespoon sun dried tomatoes
- 1 cup white sauce
- ½ cup fresh cream
- 4 cups water
- 2 teaspoons salt
- ¼ teaspoon black pepper

Directions:

1. Put the butter, onions and garlic in the Instant Pot and select "Sauté".

2. Sauté for 4 minutes and add tomato paste, spinach, salt, pepper and water.

3. Set the Instant Pot to "Soup" and cook for 10 minutes at high pressure.

4. Release the pressure naturally and add white sauce and fresh cream.

5. Blend the contents of the Instant Pot to a smooth consistency.

6. Garnish with feta cheese and sun dried tomatoes.

Nutritional Information per Serving:

Calories: 360 ; Total Fat: 28.3g; Carbs: 18.3g; Sugars: 9.7g; Protein: 9.2g;

Cholesterol: 66mg; Sodium: 2245mg

14.Chestnut Soup

Yield: 4 Servings

Total Time: 25 Minutes

Prep Time: 10 Minutes

Cook Time: 15 Minutes

Ingredients

- ½ pound fresh chestnuts

- 4 tablespoons butter

- 1 sprig sage

- ¼ teaspoon white pepper

- 4 cups chicken stock

- ¼ teaspoon nutmeg

- 1 onion, chopped

- 1 stalk celery, chopped

- 1 potato, chopped

- 2 tablespoons rum
- 2 tablespoons fresh cream

Directions:

1. Puree the fresh chestnuts in a blender.
2. Put the butter, onions, sage, celery and white pepper in the Instant Pot and select "Sauté".
3. Sauté for 4 minutes and add potato, stock and chestnuts.
4. Set the Instant Pot to "Soup" and cook for 15 minutes at high pressure.
5. Release the pressure naturally and add rum, nutmeg and fresh cream.
6. Blend the contents of the Instant Pot to a smooth consistency.

Nutritional Information per Serving:
Calories: 290; Total Fat: 13.3g; Carbs: 36.5g; Sugars: 2.5g; Protein: 3g; Cholesterol: 32mg; Sodium: 856mg

15.Tortilla and White Beans Soup

Yield: 4 Servings

Total Time: 27 Minutes

Prep Time: 10 Minutes

Cook Time: 17 Minutes

Ingredients

- 1 cup white beans
- 4 tablespoons butter
- ¼ teaspoon white pepper
- 1 onion, roughly sliced

- 1 tablespoon sun dried tomatoes
- ¼ cup fresh cream
- 4 cups water
- 2 teaspoons salt
- 1 carrot, roughly chopped
- 4 garlic cloves, minced
- 4 tablespoons tomato paste
- Crunchy tortilla chips, for garnish

Directions:

1. Put the butter, garlic, carrots, onions and white pepper in the Instant Pot and select "Sauté".
2. Sauté for 5 minutes and add white beans, potatoes, sun dried tomatoes, tomato paste, salt and water.
3. Set the Instant Pot to "Soup" and cook for 12 minutes at high pressure.
4. Release the pressure naturally and add sour cream.
5. Blend the contents of the Instant Pot to a smooth consistency and top with crunchy tortilla chips.

Nutritional Information per Serving:

Calories: 353; Total Fat: 14.7g; Carbs: 44.2g; Sugars: 5.3g; Protein: 14g; Cholesterol: 33mg; Sodium: 1337mg

16.Vegetable Noodle Soup

Yield: 5 Servings

Total Time: 20 Minutes

Prep Time: 8 Minutes

Cook Time: 12 Minutes

Ingredients

- ½ cup potatoes, diced
- ½ cup peas
- ½ cup carrots
- ½ cup cauliflower
- 6 oz. noodles, cooked and drained
- ½ cup onions
- 3 garlic cloves, minced
- ½ inch ginger, minced
- 1 cup tomatoes, diced
- 10 oz. baby carrots
- 2 teaspoons Worcestershire sauce
- 32 oz. vegetable stock
- 1 tablespoon olive oil
- 1 teaspoon salt
- 1 teaspoon black pepper

Directions:

1. Put the oil, ginger, garlic, carrots, onions and cauliflowers in the Instant Pot and select "Sauté".

2. Sauté for 5 minutes and add potatoes, tomatoes, peas, vegetable stock and Worcestershire sauce.
3. Set the Instant Pot to "Soup" and cook for 12 minutes at high pressure.
4. Release the pressure naturally and add cooked noodles.
5. Season with salt and black pepper and serve immediately.

Nutritional Information per Serving:
Calories: 148; Total Fat: 4g; Carbs: 24.8g; Sugars: 7.8g; Protein: 4.6g;

Cholesterol: 10mg; Sodium: 174mg

17.Manchow Soup

Yield: 4 Servings

Total Time: 25 Minutes

Prep Time: 10 Minutes

Cook Time: 15 Minutes

Ingredients

- 3 oz. fried noodles, for garnish
- ½ cup green bell peppers
- ½ cup bean sprouts
- ½ cup mushrooms
- ½ cup broccoli
- ½ cup baby carrots
- 2 green onions, chopped
- 4 garlic cloves, minced
- ½ inch ginger, minced

- 1 teaspoon soy sauce
- 1 teaspoon vinegar
- 2 teaspoons chilli sauce
- 3 cups vegetable stock
- 1 tablespoon oil
- Salt and pepper, to taste
- Roasted crushed peanuts, for garnish

Directions:

1. Put the oil, ginger, garlic, carrots, onions and carrots in the Instant Pot and select "Sauté".
2. Sauté for 4 minutes and add soy sauce, chilli sauce, vinegar and vegetable stock.
3. Set the Instant Pot to "Soup" and cook for 10 minutes at high pressure.
4. Release the pressure naturally and add cooked noodles.
5. Season with salt and black pepper and garnish with fried noodles and crushed roasted peanuts.

Nutritional Information per Serving:
Calories: 379; Total Fat: 20.8g; Carbs: 43.6g; Sugars: 2.4g; Protein: 8.7g; Cholesterol: 0mg; Sodium: 425mg

18.Chinese Noodle Soup

Yield: 8 Servings

Total Time: 30 Minutes

Prep Time: 10 Minutes

Cook Time: 20 Minutes

Ingredients

- 12 oz. noodles, cooked and drained
- 1 cup red bell peppers
- 1 cup mushrooms
- 1 cup broccoli
- 1 cup bokchoy
- 4 green onion whites
- 8 garlic cloves, minced
- 1 inch ginger, minced
- 2 teaspoons soy sauce
- 1 teaspoon white chilli vinegar
- 20 oz. baby carrots
- 2 teaspoons chilli sauce
- 8 cups vegetable stock
- 2 tablespoons oil
- Salt and pepper, to taste
- Onion greens, for garnish

Directions:

1. Put the oil, ginger, garlic, baby carrots and onions in the Instant Pot and select "Sauté".
2. Sauté for 4 minutes and add broccoli, bokchoy, red bell peppers,mushrooms,soy sauce, chilli vinegar, chilli sauce and vegetable stock.
3. Set the Instant Pot to "Soup" and cook for 15 minutes at high pressure.
4. Release the pressure naturally and add cooked noodles.
5. Season with salt and black pepper and garnish with onion greens.

Nutritional Information per Serving:
Calories: 145; Total Fat: 4.7g; Carbs: 22.6g; Sugars: 6.1g; Protein: 4g; Cholesterol: 12mg; Sodium: 207mg

19.Japanese Udon Noodle Soup

Yield: 2 Servings

Total Time: 27 Minutes

Prep Time: 10 Minutes

Cook Time: 17 Minutes

Ingredients

- 3 oz. Japanese udon noodles, cooked and drained
- ½ cup green bell peppers
- ½ cup celery
- ½ cup mushrooms
- ½ cup bamboo shoots
- 2 garlic cloves, minced

- ½ green chilli, finely chopped
- ½ cup baby carrots
- 1 teaspoon rice vinegar soy sauce
- 2 cups chicken stock
- ½ inch ginger, minced
- 1 green onion white
- 1 teaspoon rice wine vinegar
- 1 teaspoon red chilli sauce
- 1 tablespoon sesame oil
- Bean sprouts and green onions, for garnish
- Salt and pepper, to taste

Directions:

1. Put the oil, ginger, garlic, baby carrots and onions in the Instant Pot and select "Sauté".

2. Sauté for 4 minutes and add bamboo shoots, celery, green bell peppers,mushrooms, soy sauce, rice wine vinegar, chilli sauce and chicken stock.

3. Set the Instant Pot to "Soup" and cook for 13 minutes at high pressure.

4. Release the pressure naturally and add cooked udon noodles.

5. Season with salt and black pepper and garnish with onion greens and bean sprouts.

Nutritional Information per Serving:

Calories: 179; Total Fat: 3.9g; Carbs: 30g; Sugars: 2.7g; Protein: 3.6g;

Cholesterol: 0mg; Sodium: 473mg

20.Chestnut Bacon Soup

Yield: 4 Servings

Total Time: 34 Minutes

Prep Time: 10 Minutes

Cook Time: 24 Minutes

Ingredients

- 5 meatless bacon strips, cooked crispy
- 1 bay laurel leaf
- ½ pound fresh chestnuts
- 3 tablespoons butter
- 1 sprig sage
- ¼ teaspoon white pepper
- 4 cups chicken stock
- ¼ teaspoon nutmeg
- 1 onion, chopped
- 1 potato, chopped
- 2 tablespoons fresh cream

Directions:

1. Puree the fresh chestnuts in a blender.
2. Put the butter, onions, sage, celery and white pepper in the Instant Pot and select "Sauté".
3. Sauté for 4 minutes and add potato, bay laurel leaf, stock and chestnuts.
4. Set the Instant Pot to "Soup" and cook for 20 minutes at high pressure.
5. Release the pressure naturally and add nutmeg and fresh cream.

6. Blend the contents of the Instant Pot to a smooth consistency and serve with bacon.

Nutritional Information per Serving:
Calories: 435; Total Fat: 25.4g; Carbs: 37.7g; Sugars: 2.4g; Protein: 16.7g; Cholesterol: 62mg; Sodium: 1594mg

21.Pearl Barley Soup

Yield: 6 Servings

Total Time: 26 Minutes

Prep Time: 8 Minutes

Cook Time: 18 Minutes

Ingredients

- 1 cup all-purpose flour
- 2 onions, chopped
- 2 celery stalks, chopped
- 2 carrots, chopped
- 4 tablespoons olive oil
- 2 cups mushroom, sliced
- 28 oz. vegetable stock
- ¾ cup pearl barley
- 2 teaspoons dried oregano
- 1 cup purple wine
- Salt and pepper, to taste

Directions:

1. Put the oil, garlic and onions in the Instant Pot and select "Sauté".
2. Sauté for 3 minutes and add rest of the ingredients.
3. Set the Instant Pot to "Soup" and cook for 15 minutes at high pressure.
4. Release the pressure naturally and serve hot.

Nutritional Information per Serving:

Calories: 310; Total Fat: 10.1g; Carbs: 43.8g; Sugars: 4.2g; Protein: 6.6g; Cholesterol: 0mg; Sodium: 92mg

22.Lemon Rice Soup

Yield: 6 Servings

Total Time: 26 Minutes

Prep Time: 10 Minutes

Cook Time: 16 Minutes

Ingredients

- ¾ cup lengthy grain rice
- 1 cup onions, sliced
- 1 cup carrots, chopped
- 6 cups vegetable broth
- Salt and pepper, to taste
- ¾ cup lemon juice, freshly squeezed
- 3 teaspoons minced garlic
- 1 cup celery, chopped
- 2 tablespoons olive oil

- 2 tablespoons all-purpose flour

Directions:

1. Put the oil, garlic, celery and onions in the Instant Pot and select "Sauté".
2. Sauté for 4 minutes and add rest of the ingredients except all-purpose flour and lemon juice.
3. Set the Instant Pot to "Soup" and cook for 12 minutes at high pressure.
4. Release the pressure naturally and add the whisked lemon juice+ all-purpose flour mixture.
5. Let it simmer till the soup becomes thick and season with salt and pepper.

Nutritional Information per Serving:

Calories: 225; Total Fat: 12g; Carbs: 25.5g; Sugars: 4.9g; Protein: 5.1g; Cholesterol: 2mg; Sodium: 1032mg

23.Basil Coriander Lemon Soup

Yield: 3 Servings

Total Time: 27 Minutes

Prep Time: 10 Minutes

Cook Time: 17 Minutes

Ingredients

- ½ cup onions, sliced
- ½ cup carrots, chopped
- 16 oz. can vegetable broth
- 1/3 cup fresh coriander, chopped
- ¼ cup lemon juice, freshly squeezed

- 2 teaspoons garlic, minced
- ½ cup celery, chopped
- 2 tablespoons olive oil
- 1/3 cup fresh basil leaves, chopped
- Salt and pepper, to taste
- 2 tablespoons all-purpose flour

Directions:

1. Put the oil, garlic, celery and onions in the Instant Pot and select "Sauté".
2. Sauté for 4 minutes and add rest of the ingredients except all-purpose flour and lemon juice.
3. Set the Instant Pot to "Soup" and cook for 13 minutes at high pressure.
4. Release the pressure naturally and add the whisked lemon juice and all-purpose flour mixture.
5. Let it simmer till the soup becomes thick and season with salt and pepper.

Nutritional Information per Serving:

Calories: 135; Total Fat: 9.6g; Carbs: 11.2g; Sugars: 3.7g; Protein: 1.4g; Cholesterol: 0mg; Sodium: 366mg

24.Beetroot Soup

Yield: 4 Servings

Total Time: 30 Minutes

Prep Time: 10 Minutes

Cook Time: 20 Minutes

Ingredients

- 2 pounds beetroot, peeled and diced

- 3 teaspoons garlic, minced
- ½ cup onions, sliced
- ½ cup celery, chopped
- ½ cup carrots, chopped
- 3 tablespoons olive oil
- 4 cups vegetable broth
- 3 tablespoons fresh coriander, chopped
- Salt and pepper, to taste
- 3 tablespoons fresh cream

Directions:

1. Put the oil, garlic, celery and onions in the Instant Pot and select "Sauté".
2. Sauté for 4 minutes and add rest of the ingredients except fresh cream.
3. Set the Instant Pot to "Soup" and cook for 16 minutes at high pressure.
4. Release the pressure naturally and add the fresh cream.
5. Season with salt and pepper and garnish with coriander leaves.

Nutritional Information per Serving:

Calories: 251; Total Fat: 12.8g; Carbs: 27.6g; Sugars: 20.4g; Protein: 9.2g; Cholesterol: 2mg; Sodium: 962mg

25.Lentil and Smoked Paprika Soup

Yield: 10 Servings

Total Time: 21 Minutes

Prep Time: 10 Minutes

Cook Time: 11 Minutes

Ingredients

- 2 cups red lentils, rinsed
- 2cups green lentils, rinse
- 1½ pounds potatoes
- 1½ bunches rainbow chard
- 2 onions, chopped finely
- 4 teaspoons cumin
- 2teaspoons salt
- 2 celery stalks
- 6 garlic cloves, minced
- 3 teaspoons smoked paprika
- 4 carrots, sliced
- 10 cups water
- Salt and pepper, to taste

Directions:

1. Put the oil, garlic, celery and onions in the Instant Pot and select "Sauté".
2. Sauté for 4 minutes and add rest of the ingredients except lentils.
3. Set the Instant Pot to "Soup" and cook for 7 minutes at high pressure.
4. Release the pressure naturally and add season with salt and pepper.

Nutritional Information per Serving:

Calories: 209; Total Fat: 0.8g; Carbs: 39.6g; Sugars: 3.9g; Protein: 11.9g;

Cholesterol: 0mg; Sodium: 501mg

Nutritional Vegetables Recipes

26.Brussels Sprout Salad

Yield: 4 Servings

Total Time: 15 Minutes

Prep Time: 10 Minutes

Cook Time: 5 Minutes

Ingredients

- 1 pound Brussels sprouts, trimmed and halved
- 1 cup pomegranate seeds
- ¼ cup cashew nuts, chopped
- ½ tablespoon unsalted butter, melted
- ¼ cup almonds, chopped
- 1 cup water
- Salt and black pepper, to taste

Directions

1. Place the steamer trivet in the bottom of Instant Pot and add water.
2. Put the Brussels sprout on the trivet.
3. Set the Instant Pot to "Manual" at high pressure for 4 minutes.
4. Release the pressure naturally and top with melted butter, almonds, cashew nuts and pomegranate seeds.

Nutritional Information per Serving:

Calories: 170; Total Fat: 8.8g; Carbs: 20.4g; Sugars: 6.1g; Protein: 6.7g; Cholesterol: 4mg; Sodium: 42mg

27.Whole Garlic Roast

Yield: 4 Servings

Total Time: 11 Minutes

Prep Time: 2 Minutes

Cook Time: 9 Minutes

Ingredients

- 4 large garlic bulbs
- 2 tablespoons herbed butter
- 1 cup water
- Salt and black pepper, to taste

Directions

1. Place the steamer trivet in the bottom of Instant Pot and add water.
2. Season the garlic bulbs with salt and pepper.
3. Put the seasoned garlic bulbs on the trivet.
4. Set the Instant Pot to "Manual" at high pressure for 6 minutes.
5. Release the pressure naturally and remove the trivet.
6. Put the herbed butter and garlic bulbs and select "Sauté".
7. Sauté for 3 minutes and dish out.

Nutritional Information per Serving:

Calories: 66; Total Fat: 5.8g; Carbs: 3g; Sugars: 0g; Protein: 0.1g; Cholesterol: 15mg; Sodium: 43mg

28.Tangy Lemon Potatoes

Yield: 6 Servings

Total Time: 15 Minutes

Prep Time: 3 Minutes

Cook Time: 12 Minutes

Ingredients

- 10 medium potatoes, scrubbed and cubed
- 4 tablespoons fresh lemon juice
- 2 tablespoons olive oil
- 4 tablespoons fresh rosemary, chopped
- 2 cups vegetable broth
- Salt and black pepper, to taste

Directions:

1. Put the olive oil and potatoes in the Instant Pot and select "Sauté".
2. Sauté for 4 minutes and add the rosemary, salt and black pepper.
3. Sauté for 2 minutes and stir in the lemon juice and broth.
4. Set the Instant Pot to "Manual" at high pressure for 6 minutes.
5. Release the pressure naturally and serve warm.

Nutritional Information per Serving:

Calories: 307; Total Fat: 5.9g; Carbs: 57.7g; Sugars: 4.5g; Protein: 7.8g;

Cholesterol: 0mg; Sodium: 279mg

29.Caramelised Onions

Yield: 2 Servings

Total Time: 12 Minutes

Prep Time: 3 Minutes

Cook Time: 9 Minutes

Ingredients

- 3 large onion bulbs
- 1 cup water
- 1 tablespoon butter
- Salt and black pepper, to taste

Directions:

1. Place the steamer trivet in the bottom of Instant Pot and add water.
2. Season the onion bulbs with salt and pepper.
3. Put the seasoned onion bulbs on the trivet.
4. Set the Instant Pot to "Manual" at high pressure for 6 minutes.
5. Release the pressure naturally and remove the trivet.
6. Put the butter and garlic bulbs and select "Sauté".
7. Sauté for 3 minutes and dish out.

Nutritional Information per Serving:
Calories: 63; Total Fat: 5.8g; Carbs: 2.8g; Sugars: 0.9g; Protein: 0.8g;

Cholesterol: 0mg; Sodium: 50mg

30.Tomato Sauce Spinach

Yield: 4 Servings

Total Time: 18 Minutes

Prep Time: 5 Minutes

Cook Time: 13 Minutes

Ingredients

- 1 tablespoon olive oil
- 1 small onion, chopped
- 1 teaspoon garlic, minced
- ½ teaspoon red pepper flakes, crushed
- 5 cups fresh spinach, chopped
- ½ cup tomatoes, chopped
- ¼ cup homemade tomato puree
- ¼ cup white wine
- ½ cup vegetable broth

Directions:

1. Put the olive oil and onions in the Instant Pot and select "Sauté".
2. Sauté for 4 minutes and add garlic, spinach and red pepper flakes.
3. Sauté for 3 minutes and stir in the remaining ingredients.
4. Set the Instant Pot to "Manual" at high pressure for 6 minutes.
5. Release the pressure quickly and serve warm.

Nutritional Information per Serving:

Calories: 72; Total Fat: 3.9g; Carbs: 5.5g; Sugars: 2.2g; Protein: 2.3g;

Cholesterol: 0mg; Sodium: 130mg

31. Steamed Tomatoes

Yield: 4 Servings

Total Time: 10 Minutes

Prep Time: 3 Minutes

Cook Time: 7 Minutes

Ingredients

- 4 large tomatoes
- 1 cup water
- 1 tablespoon herbed butter
- 1 cup mozzarella cheese, shredded

Directions:

1. Place the steamer trivet in the bottom of Instant Pot and add water.
2. Scoop out the inner filling of the tomato and stuff with the mozzarella cheese.
3. Put the stuffed tomatoes on the trivet.
4. Set the Instant Pot to "Manual" at high pressure for 5 minutes.
5. Release the pressure naturally and remove the trivet.
6. Put the herbed butter and stuffed tomatoes and select "Sauté".
7. Sauté for 2 minutes and dish out.

Nutritional Information per Serving:

Calories: 75; Total Fat: 3.2g; Carbs: 7.5g; Sugars: 4.9g; Protein: 5g; Cholesterol: 10mg; Sodium: 71mg

32.Glazed Carrots

Yield: 3 Servings

Total Time: 10 Minutes

Prep Time: 5 Minutes

Cook Time: 5 Minutes

Ingredients

- 1 pound carrots, peeled and sliced diagonally
- ½ cup water
- 1 tablespoon honey
- ¼ cup golden raisins
- 1 tablespoon unsalted butter, melted
- ½ teaspoon red pepper flakes, crushed
- Pinch of salt

Directions

1. Put the carrots, water and raisins in the Instant Pot.
2. Set the Instant Pot to "Manual" at low pressure for 5 minutes.
3. Release the pressure naturally and transfer he carrots into a bowl.
4. Stir in the remaining ingredients and mix well to serve.

Nutritional Information per Serving:

Calories: 154; Total Fat: 4g; Carbs: 30.4g; Sugars: 20.4g; Protein: 1.7g;

Cholesterol: 10mg; Sodium: 134mg

33.Rosemary Baby Potatoes

Yield: 7 Servings

Total Time: 20 Minutes

Prep Time: 5 Minutes

Cook Time: 15 Minutes

Ingredients

- 20 baby potatoes
- 2 cups water
- 1 cup fresh rosemary
- 4tablespoons herb butter

Directions:

1. Place the steamer trivet in the bottom of Instant Pot and add water.
2. Put the baby potatoes and rosemary on the trivet.
3. Set the Instant Pot to "Manual" at high pressure for 10 minutes.
4. Release the pressure naturally and remove the trivet.
5. Put the herbed butter and baby potatoes and select "Sauté".
6. Sauté for 5 minutes and dish out.

Nutritional Information per Serving:

Calories: 108; Total Fat: 1.7g; Carbs: 22.1g; Sugars: 0g; Protein: 3.6g; Cholesterol: 1mg; Sodium: 77mg

34.Chili Polenta

Yield: 6 Servings

Total Time: 15 Minutes

Prep Time: 5 Minutes

Cook Time: 10 Minutes

Ingredients

- 3 cups coarse polenta
- 10 cups water
- 3 teaspoons salt
- 3tablespoons red paprika flakes

Directions:

1. Put the water, salt, red paprika flakes and polenta flour in the Instant Pot.

2. Set the Instant Pot to "Manual" at high pressure for 9 minutes.

3. Release the pressure naturally and dish out.

Nutritional Information per Serving:

Calories: 310; Total Fat: 9.7g; Carbs: 66.8g; Sugars: 0.8g; Protein: 5.8g;

Cholesterol: 0mg; Sodium: 1178mg

35.Steamed Cabbage Sheets

Yield: 4 Servings

Total Time: 15 Minutes

Prep Time: 6 Minutes

Cook Time: 9 Minutes

Ingredients

- 12 sheets of fresh cabbage
- 3 teaspoons fresh basil
- 3 teaspoons olive oil
- 2 cups water
- Salt and pepper

Directions:

1. Place the steamer trivet in the bottom of Instant Pot and add water.
2. Put the cabbage sheets and basil on the trivet.
3. Set the Instant Pot to "Manual" at high pressure for 6 minutes.
4. Release the pressure naturally and remove the trivet.
5. Put the olive oil, cabbage sheets, salt and black pepper and select "Sauté".
6. Sauté for 3 minutes and dish out.

Nutritional Information per Serving:

Calories: 55; Total Fat: 3.6g; Carbs: 5.8g; Sugars: 3.2g; Protein: 1.3g;

Cholesterol: 0mg; Sodium: 21mg

36.Instant Pot Corn Kernels

Yield: 4 Servings

Total Time: 13 Minutes

Prep Time: 5 Minutes

Cook Time: 8 Minutes

Ingredients

- 1½ cups corn kernels
- 2 cups water
- 1 tablespoons lemon juice
- 2 tablespoons butter
- 1 teaspoon red pepper powder
- Salt and black pepper, to taste

Directions:

1. Season the corn kernels with red pepper powder, salt and black pepper
2. Place the steamer trivet in the bottom of Instant Pot and add water.
3. Put the seasoned corn kernels on the trivet.
4. Set the Instant Pot to "Manual" at high pressure for 5 minutes.
5. Release the pressure naturally and remove the trivet.
6. Put the butter and corn kernels and select "Sauté".
7. Sauté for 3 minutes and stir in the lemon juice.

Nutritional Information per Serving:
Calories: 188; Total Fat: 6.7g; Carbs: 32.2g; Sugars: 5.6g; Protein: 5.6g;

Cholesterol: 12mg; Sodium: 67mg

37.Steamed French and Broad Beans

Yield: 6 Servings

Total Time: 23 Minutes

Prep Time: 5 Minutes

Cook Time: 18 Minutes

Ingredients

- 1 cup French beans, washed
- 1 cup broad beans, washed
- 1 teaspoon ginger powder
- 3 cups water
- 3 tablespoons olive oil
- Salt and black pepper, to taste

Directions:

1. Season the French beans and broad beans with ginger powder, salt and black pepper
2. Place the steamer trivet in the bottom of Instant Pot and add water.
3. Put the seasoned beans on the trivet.
4. Set the Instant Pot to "Manual" at high pressure for 12 minutes.
5. Release the pressure naturally and remove the trivet.
6. Put the olive oil and beans and select "Sauté".
7. Sauté for 5 minutes and stir in the lemon juice.

Nutritional Information per Serving:

Calories: 260; Total Fat: 8g; Carbs: 37.2g; Sugars: 0.7g; Protein: 11.1g;

Cholesterol: 0mg; Sodium: 13mg

38.Thai Sweet Potatoes

Yield: 5 Servings

Total Time: 15 Minutes

Prep Time: 5 Minutes

Cook Time: 10 Minutes

Ingredients

- 3 cups sweet potatoes
- 1 tablespoon butter
- 1 cup water
- ¼ cup Thai red sauce
- 1 tablespoon brown sugar
- 1½ cups brown rice, cooked
- ½ cup pecans, chopped
- ¾ cup cheddar cheese, shredded

Directions:

1. Put the water and sweet potatoes in the Instant Pot.
2. Set the Instant Pot to "Manual" at high pressure for 7 minutes.
3. Release the pressure naturally and add rest of the ingredients except rice and cheese.
4. Let it simmer for 3 minutes and dish out over the cooked rice.
5. Garnish with shredded cheddar cheese and serve.

Nutritional Information per Serving:

Calories: 441; Total Fat: 12.7g; Carbs: 71.5g; Sugars: 2.7g; Protein: 10.4g; Cholesterol: 24mg; Sodium: 195mg

39.Mixed Veggies

Yield: 3 Servings

Total Time: 22 Minutes

Prep Time: 10 Minutes

Cook Time: 12 Minutes

Ingredients

- 1 tablespoon olive oil
- 8 oz. mushrooms, sliced
- 1 zucchini, sliced
- 1 bell pepper, diced
- 1 Japanese eggplant, peeled and sliced
- 1 medium potato, peeled and diced
- 1 small onion, thinly sliced
- 1 garlic clove, minced
- 1 tablespoon tomato paste
- 1 teaspoon oregano
- 1 teaspoon basil
- 3 tablespoons water
- ¼ teaspoon red pepper flakes
- ½ cup Parmigiano-Reggiano cheese, grated
- Salt and pepper, to taste

Directions:

1. Put the olive oil, onions, garlic and potatoes in the Instant Pot and select "Sauté".

2. Sauté for 3 minutes and add rest of the ingredients except cheese.

3. Set the Instant Pot to "Manual" at high pressure for 10 minutes.

4. Release the pressure naturally and add Parmigiano-Reggiano cheese.

Nutritional Information per Serving:
Calories: 212; Total Fat: 6.6g; Carbs: 34.9g; Sugars: 12.2g; Protein: 8.9g;
Cholesterol: 3mg; Sodium: 70mg

40.Delicious Succotash

Yield: 6 Servings

Total Time: 20 Minutes

Prep Time: 7 Minutes

Cook Time: 13 Minutes

Ingredients

- 1 cup bell peppers

- 2 cups complete corn kernels

- 2 cups water

- 3 tablespoons butter

- 2 cups lima beans

- 2 cups tomatoes

- 2 teaspoons salt

Directions:

1. Put the butter and bell peppers in the Instant Pot and select "Sauté".

2. Sauté for 3 minutes and add rest of the ingredients.

3. Set the Instant Pot to "Manual" at high pressure for 10 minutes.

4. Release the pressure naturally and serve hot.

Nutritional Information per Serving:
Calories: 153; Total Fat: 6.7g; Carbs: 19.7g; Sugars: 5.4g; Protein: 5g;
Cholesterol: 15mg; Sodium: 929mg

41.Vegetable Medley

Yield: 3 Servings

Total Time: 14 Minutes

Prep Time: 5 Minutes

Cook Time: 9 Minutes

Ingredients

- 1 small sweet potato, peeled and diced
- 2 carrots, peeled and diced
- 3 pink potatoes, quartered
- 1½ cups butternut squash
- 1 tablespoon olive oil
- 1 sprig rosemary
- ½ cup water
- Salt and pepper, to taste

Directions:

1. Put the olive oil and rosemary sprig in the Instant Pot and select "Sauté".
2. Sauté for 2 minutes and add rest of the ingredients.
3. Set the Instant Pot to "Manual" at high pressure for 7 minutes.
4. Release the pressure naturally and serve hot.

Nutritional Information per Serving:
Calories: 202; Total Fat: 5.2g; Carbs: 40.6g; Sugars: 9g; Protein: 3.6g;

Cholesterol: 0mg; Sodium: 48mg

42.Couscous Stuffed Peppers

Yield: 4 Servings

Total Time: 46 Minutes

Prep Time: 10 Minutes

Cook Time: 36 Minutes

Ingredients

- 1 cup couscous
- 4 tablespoons pine nuts, roasted
- 4 large red bell peppers
- 2 cups water
- 2 teaspoons dried oregano
- 1 teaspoon salt
- ½ teaspoon black pepper
- ¼ cup feta cheese, crumbled

Directions:

1. Put the water and couscous in the Instant Pot.
2. Set the Instant Pot to "Manual" at high pressure for 3 minutes.
3. Release the pressure naturally and add rest of the ingredients.
4. Sauté for 3 minutes and fill this stuffing evenly in the bell peppers.
5. Bake in a pre-heated oven at 375°F for 30 minutes.

Nutritional Information per Serving:
Calories: 286; Total Fat: 8.6g; Carbs: 44.6g; Sugars: 6.7g; Protein: 9.3g; Cholesterol: 8mg; Sodium: 697mg

43.Spicy Cauliflower

Yield: 3 Servings

Total Time: 15 Minutes

Prep Time: 10 Minutes

Cook Time: 5 Minutes

Ingredients

- 1 pound cauliflower
- ½ cup vegetable broth
- 1 tablespoon fresh lemon juice
- 1 tablespoon olive oil
- 1 teaspoon red pepper flakes, crushed
- Salt, to taste

Directions:

1. Season the cauliflower with salt and red pepper flakes.
2. Put the olive oil and cauliflowers in the Instant Pot and select "Sauté".
3. Sauté for 4 minutes and add vegetable broth.
4. Set the Instant Pot to "Manual" at high pressure for 6 minutes.
5. Release the pressure naturally and stir in the lemon juice.

Nutritional Information per Serving:

Calories: 87; Total Fat: 5.2g; Carbs: 8.6g; Sugars: 3.9g; Protein: 3.9g; Cholesterol: 0mg; Sodium: 174mg

44.Nutty Brussels Sprouts

Yield: 3 Servings

Total Time: 9 Minutes

Prep Time: 5 Minutes

Cook Time: 4 Minutes

Ingredients

- 1 pound brussels sprouts, trimmed and halved
- ½ tablespoon butter, melted
- ½ cup almonds, chopped
- 1 teaspoon salt

Directions:

1. Place the steamer trivet in the bottom of Instant Pot and add water.
2. Put the brussels sprouts on the trivet.
3. Set the Instant Pot to "Manual" at high pressure for 4 minutes.
4. Release the pressure quickly and remove the trivet.
5. Drizzle with butter and top with almonds.

Nutritional Information per Serving:

Calories: 174; Total Fat: 10.4g; Carbs: 17.1g; Sugars: 3.9g; Protein: 8.5g; Cholesterol: 5mg; Sodium: 52mg

45.Simple Broccoli

Yield: 3 Servings

Total Time: 10 Minutes

Prep Time: 5 Minutes

Cook Time: 5 Minutes

Ingredients

- 1 pound broccoli florets

- 1 cup water

- 2 tablespoons butter, melted

- Salt and freshly ground black pepper, to taste

Directions:

1. Place the steamer trivet in the bottom of Instant Pot and add water.

2. Put the broccoli florets on the trivet.

3. Set the Instant Pot to "Manual" at high pressure for 5 minutes.

4. Release the pressure quickly and remove the trivet.

5. Drizzle with butter and season with salt and black pepper.

Nutritional Information per Serving:

Calories: 119; Total Fat: 8.2g; Carbs: 10.1g; Sugars: 2.6g; Protein: 4.3g;

Cholesterol: 20mg; Sodium: 104mg

46.Refreshing Green Beans

Yield: 6 Servings

Total Time: 11 Minutes

Prep Time: 5 Minutes

Cook Time: 6 Minutes

Ingredients

- 2 pounds fresh green beans
- 2 garlic cloves, minced
- 4 tablespoons butter
- 3 cups water
- Salt and freshly ground black pepper, to taste

Directions:

1. Put the fresh green beans and all other ingredients in the Instant Pot.
2. Set the Instant Pot to "Manual" at high pressure for 6 minutes.
3. Release the pressure quickly and serve hot.

Nutritional Information per Serving:

Calories: 116; Total Fat: 7.9g; Carbs: 11.1g; Sugars: 2.1g; Protein: 2.9g;

Cholesterol: 20mg; Sodium: 64mg

47.Kale and Carrots Platter

Yield: 4 Servings

Total Time: 22 Minutes

Prep Time: 5 Minutes

Cook Time: 17 Minutes

Ingredients

- 1 cup fresh kale, trimmed and chopped
- 3 medium carrots, peeled and cut into ½-inch slices
- 5 garlic cloves, minced
- 2tablespoons olive oil
- 1 small onion, chopped
- ½ cup vegetable broth
- 1 tablespoon fresh lemon juice
- ¼ teaspoon red pepper flakes, crushed
- Salt and black pepper, to taste

Directions:

1. Put the olive oil, garlic and onions in the Instant Pot and select "Sauté".
2. Sauté for 4 minutes and add carrots.
3. Sauté for 3 minutes and add broth, kale, red pepper flakes, salt and black pepper.
4. Set the Instant Pot to "Manual" at high pressure for 9 minutes.
5. Release the pressure naturally and stir in the lemon juice.

Nutritional Information per Serving:

Calories: 103; Total Fat: 7.1g; Carbs: 9.7g; Sugars: 3.4g; Protein: 1.4g; Cholesterol: 0mg; Sodium: 107mg

48.Healthy Spinach Plate

Yield: 3 Servings

Total Time: 19 Minutes

Prep Time: 5 Minutes

Cook Time: 14 Minutes

Ingredients

- 5 cups fresh spinach, chopped
- 1 small onion, chopped
- 1 cup vegetable broth
- 1 tablespoon garlic, minced
- 1tablespoon olive oil
- 1 tablespoon fresh lemon juice
- ½ cup tomatoes, chopped
- ½ cup tomato puree
- ½ teaspoon red pepper flakes, crushed
- Salt and freshly ground black pepper, to taste

Directions:

1. Put the olive oil, garlic and onions in the Instant Pot and select "Sauté".
2. Sauté for 4 minutes and add spinach, red pepper flakes, salt and black pepper.
3. Sauté for 3 minutes and add in the remaining ingredients.
4. Set the Instant Pot to "Manual" at high pressure for 7 minutes.
5. Release the pressure quickly and serve hot.

Nutritional Information per Serving:

Calories: 101 ; Total Fat: 5.6g; Carbs: 10.4g; Sugars: 4.4g; Protein: 4.5g; Cholesterol: 0mg; Sodium: 310mg

49.Colorful Veggies

Yield: 8 Servings

Total Time: 18 Minutes

Prep Time: 5 Minutes

Cook Time: 13 Minutes

Ingredients

- 1½ pounds cherry tomatoes
- 8 medium zucchinis, chopped roughly
- 2 tablespoons olive oil
- 3 garlic cloves, minced
- 3 small yellow onions, chopped roughly
- 1½ cups water
- 3 tablespoons fresh basil, chopped
- Salt and black pepper, to taste

Directions:

1. Put the olive oil, garlic and onions in the Instant Pot and select "Sauté".
2. Sauté for 4 minutes and add zucchinis and tomatoes.
3. Sauté for 3 minutes and add remaining ingredients except basil.
4. Set the Instant Pot to "Manual" at high pressure for 6 minutes.
5. Release the pressure naturally and garnish with basil.

Nutritional Information per Serving:

Calories: 130; Total Fat: 4.5g; Carbs: 21.6g; Sugars: 12.7g; Protein: 5.5g; Cholesterol: 0mg; Sodium: 41mg

50.Vegetables Casserole

Yield: 6 Servings

Total Time: 45 Minutes

Prep Time: 15 Minutes

Cook Time: 30 Minutes

Ingredients

- 2 medium green bell pepper, seeded and chopped
- 2 cups tomatoes, chopped
- 2 medium zucchinis, chopped
- 16 large eggs
- 1 cup almond flour
- 1cup almond milk
- 1½ cups mozzarella cheese, shredded
- Salt and black pepper, to taste

Directions:

1. Place the steamer trivet in the bottom of Instant Pot and add water.
2. Mix together almond flour, almond milk, eggs, salt and black pepper in a bowl.
3. Beat well and add vegetables and cheese.
4. Put the bowlon the trivet and close the lid.
5. Set the Instant Pot to "Manual" at high pressure for 25 minutes.
6. Release the pressure naturally and dish out.

Nutritional Information per Serving:

Calories: 443; Total Fat: 33.7g; Carbs: 15g; Sugars: 7.7g; Protein: 25.4g; Cholesterol: 500mg; Sodium: 246mg

Flavorful Rice, Beans and Lentils Recipes

51.Kidney Beans with Veggies

Yield: 4 Servings

Total Time: 55 Minutes

Prep Time: 10 Minutes

Cook Time: 45 Minutes

Ingredients

- 1 cup kidney beans, soaked overnight
- 1 medium carrot, chopped
- 1 cup tomatoes, chopped
- 3 tablespoons fresh basil
- 1 teaspoon thyme
- 1teaspoon red pepper flakes
- 1 small onion, sliced
- 3 garlic cloves, minced
- 1 tablespoon olive oil
- 1 teaspoon oregano
- Salt and black pepper, to taste

Directions:

1. Put the olive oil, garlic and onions in the Instant Pot and select "Sauté".
2. Sauté for 4 minutes and add red pepper flakes,oregano,fresh basil, thyme, salt and black pepper.
3. Sauté for 1 minute and add tomatoes, carrots, water and kidney beans.
4. Set the Instant Pot to "Manual" at high pressure for 40 minutes.

5. Release the pressure quickly and dish out.

Nutritional Information per Serving:
Calories: 213; Total Fat: 4.3g; Carbs: 34.5g; Sugars: 3.7g; Protein: 11.4g;

Cholesterol: 0mg; Sodium: 20mg

52.Black Beans Dip

Yield: 6 Servings

Total Time: 30 Minutes

Prep Time: 5 Minutes

Cook Time: 25 Minutes

Ingredients

- 2 cups black beans, soaked overnight

- 4 cups water

- 2 small onions, sliced

- 6 garlic cloves, minced

- 2 tablespoons olive oil

- 2 cups tomatoes

- 2 teaspoons chilli powder

- 1teaspoon dried oregano

- 2 cups Monterey Jack cheese, shredded

- Salt and black pepper, to taste

Directions:

1. Put all the ingredients in the Instant Pot.

2. Set the Instant Pot to "Manual" at high pressure for 20 minutes.

3. Release the pressure naturally and put the mixture in a blender.

4. Blend thoroughly and serve.

Nutritional Information per Serving:
Calories: 432; Total Fat: 17.4g; Carbs: 47g; Sugars: 4.2g; Protein: 24.4g;

Cholesterol: 34mg; Sodium: 214mg

53.Parsley in Chickpeas

Yield: 3 Servings

Total Time: 35 Minutes

Prep Time: 10 Minutes

Cook Time: 25 Minutes

Ingredients

- ½ cup chickpeas, soaked overnight

- 4 cups water

- 1 small onion, sliced

- 2 garlic cloves, minced

- 2 tablespoons olive oil

- ¼ cup parsley, chopped

- ¼ cup dill leaves, chopped

- 2 tablespoons fresh lemon juice

- 1 teaspoon salt

Directions:

1. Put water and chickpeas in the Instant Pot.

2. Set the Instant Pot to "Manual" at high pressure for 25 minutes.

3. Release the pressure naturally and put the mixture in a blender.

4. Add rest of the ingredients and blend thoroughly.

Nutritional Information per Serving:
Calories: 228; Total Fat: 11.7g; Carbs: 25.8g; Sugars: 4.8g; Protein: 7.9g;

Cholesterol: 0mg; Sodium: 32mg

54. Kidney Beans Curry

Yield: 3 Servings

Total Time: 35 Minutes

Prep Time: 10 Minutes

Cook Time: 25 Minutes

Ingredients

- 1 cup dried red kidney beans, soaked for overnight and drained
- ¼ cup split chickpeas, soaked for overnight and drained
- 4 cups water
- 3 tablespoons olive oil
- 3 teaspoons garlic, minced
- 1 large tomato, chopped finely
- 2 medium onions, chopped
- 3 teaspoons fresh ginger, minced
- 1½ teaspoons ground coriander
- 1½ teaspoons ground turmeric
- 1½ teaspoons ground cumin
- 2 teaspoons red chilli powder

- ¼ teaspoon salt
- 4 tablespoons fresh cilantro, chopped

Directions:

1. Put the olive oil, garlic, ginger and onions in the Instant Pot and select "Sauté".
2. Sauté for 4 minutes and add ground coriander, ground turmeric, ground cumin, red chilli powder and salt.
3. Sauté for 4 minutes and add water, tomatoes, beans and split chickpeas
4. Set the Instant Pot to "Manual" at high pressure for 20 minutes.
5. Release the pressure naturally and garnish with fresh cilantro.

Nutritional Information per Serving:

Calories: 427; Total Fat: 17.5g; Carbs: 64.4g; Sugars: 8.2g; Protein: 20g; Cholesterol: 0mg; Sodium: 247mg

55.Chickpeas Curry

Yield: 6 Servings

Total Time: 35 Minutes

Prep Time: 10 Minutes

Cook Time: 25 Minutes

Ingredients

- 2 cups dried chickpeas, soaked overnight
- 4 medium tomatoes, chopped finely
- 2 tablespoons olive oil
- 2 onions, chopped

- 4 cups water
- 2 tablespoons fresh ginger, minced
- 2 tablespoons garlic, minced
- 2 teaspoons curry powder
- 2 teaspoons ground cumin
- 1 teaspoon ground coriander
- ½ teaspoon salt
- ½ teaspoon black pepper, to taste
- ½ cup fresh parsley, chopped

Directions:

1. Put the oil and onions in the Instant Pot and select "Sauté".
2. Sauté for 3 minutes and add garlic, ginger, curry powder, ground cumin, ground coriander, salt and black pepper.
3. Sauté for 2 minutes and add tomatoes, chickpeas and water.
4. Set the Instant Pot to "Manual" at high pressure for 20 minutes.
5. Release the pressure naturally and garnish with parsley.

Nutritional Information per Serving:

Calories: 330; Total Fat: 9.3g; Carbs: 50.4g; Sugars: 11g; Protein: 14.7g; Cholesterol: 0mg; Sodium: 226mg

56.Lemon and Cheese Rice

Yield: 4 Servings

Total Time: 10 Minutes

Prep Time: 5 Minutes

Cook Time: 5 Minutes

Ingredients

- 2 cups white rice, rinsed
- 6 tablespoons fresh lemon juice
- 2 cups vegetable broth
- 4 tablespoons Parmesan cheese, grated freshly
- 2 teaspoons fresh lemon zest, grated finely
- 4 tablespoons fresh mint leaves, chopped
- Salt and black pepper, to taste

Directions

1. Put the rice, vegetable broth, lemon juice, salt and black pepper in the Instant Pot.
2. Set the Instant Pot to "Manual" at high pressure for 4 minutes.
3. Release the pressure naturally and then do the quick release.
4. Stir in the cheese and lemon zest and garnish with mint.

Nutritional Information per Serving:

Calories: 374; Total Fat: 2.1g; Carbs: 75.7g; Sugars: 1g; Protein: 10.2g; Cholesterol: 2mg; Sodium: 416mg

57.Quinoa Pilaf

Yield: 8 Servings

Total Time: 8 Minutes

Prep Time: 5 Minutes

Cook Time: 3 Minutes

Ingredients

- 3 cups quinoa, rinsed and drained
- 2 tablespoons butter
- 1 cup onions, chopped
- 1 cup almonds, sliced
- ½ cup dried cherries
- 2 cups chicken broth
- ½ cup water
- 2 celery stalks, chopped finely

Directions

1. Put the butter, celery, garlic and onions in the Instant Pot and select "Sauté".
2. Sauté for 4 minutes and add rest of the ingredients except almonds.
3. Set the Instant Pot to "Manual" at high pressure for 2 minutes.
4. Release the pressure quickly and stir in the almonds.

Nutritional Information per Serving:
Calories: 388; Total Fat: 13.1g; Carbs: 55.6g; Sugars: 1.3g; Protein: 13.1g; Cholesterol: 8mg; Sodium: 226mg

58.Barley and Mushrooms

Yield: 5 Servings

Total Time: 35 Minutes

Prep Time: 5 Minutes

Cook Time: 30 Minutes

Ingredients

- ¾ cup pearl barley
- ¾ pound fresh mushrooms, sliced
- 2 tablespoons olive oil, divided
- 1 garlic clove, minced
- 1 medium onion, chopped
- 1 tablespoon fresh thyme, chopped
- 2 cups chicken broth
- 1 tablespoon fresh cilantro, chopped
- ¼ cup Parmesan cheese, grated
- Salt and black pepper, to taste

Directions:

1. Put the olive oil, garlic and onions in the Instant Pot and select "Sauté".
2. Sauté for 4 minutes and add barley, thyme and chicken broth.
3. Set the Instant Pot to "Manual" at high pressure for 20 minutes.
4. Release the pressure quickly and add the mushrooms, salt and black pepper.
5. Cook for 10 minutes and add Parmesan cheese.
6. Dish out and garnish with fresh cilantro.

Nutritional Information per Serving:

Calories: 199; Total Fat: 7.1g; Carbs: 28.6g; Sugars: 2.6g; Protein: 7.8g; Cholesterol: 1mg; Sodium: 326mg

59.Green Gram Lentil Curry

Yield: 4 Servings

Total Time: 25 Minutes

Prep Time: 5 Minutes

Cook Time: 20 Minutes

Ingredients

- 1½cups green gram lentils whole, rinsed
- 1tablespoon garlic, minced
- 1½ tablespoons lemon juice
- 1½ tablespoons ginger, minced
- 4 cups water
- 1½ teaspoons salt
- 1½ teaspoons cumin seeds
- 3 medium tomatoes, chopped
- 1½tablespoons oil
- 2 medium onions, diced
- Cilantro, to garnish

Directions:

1. Put the oil, cumin seeds, garlic and onions in the Instant Pot and select "Sauté".

2. Sauté for 4 minutes and add tomato, lentils, water and spices.

3. Set the instant pot to "Manual" and cook for 15 minutes at high pressure.

4. Release the pressure naturally and add lime juice and cilantro.

Nutritional Information per Serving:
Calories: 354; Total Fat: 6.5g; Carbs: 54.8g; Sugars: 6.5g; Protein: 20.6g;
Cholesterol: 0mg; Sodium: 896mg

60.Chickpea, White Bean and Tomato Stew

Yield: 4 Servings

Total Time: 40 Minutes

Prep Time: 10 Minutes

Cook Time: 30 Minutes

Ingredients

- 1 cup dried white beans, soaked overnight

- 1 cup dried chickpeas, soaked overnight

- ¼ cup dried red lentils

- 1 medium yellow onion, chopped

- 1½ cups tomatoes, diced

- 2 tablespoons tomato paste

- 2 tablespoons olive oil

- 2 stalks celery, thinly sliced

- 2 teaspoons dried dill

- 2 teaspoons ground cinnamon

- 2 tablespoons mild paprika

- 2 teaspoons ground cumin

- 1 teaspoon salt
- 1 teaspoon ground black pepper
- 3 cups vegetable broth

Directions:

1. Put the olive oil,celery and onions in the Instant Pot and select "Sauté".
2. Sauté for 4 minutes and add dill, cinnamon, paprika, cumin, salt and black pepper.
3. Sauté for 2 minutes and add chickpeas, beans, tomatoes, lentils and tomato paste.
4. Set the instant pot to "Manual" and cook for 20 minutes at high pressure.
5. Release the pressure naturally and serve hot.

Nutritional Information per Serving:
Calories: 532; Total Fat: 12.6g; Carbs: 79.6g; Sugars: 11.6g; Protein: 30.4g; Cholesterol: 0mg; Sodium: 1198mg

61.Spinach Lentil

Yield: 3 Servings

Total Time: 15 Minutes

Prep Time: 10 Minutes

Cook Time: 5 Minutes

Ingredients

- 1 cup spinach, chopped
- ½cup split pigeon pea, washed
- ¼ teaspoon cumin seeds

- 2 garlic cloves, finely chopped
- 1½ cups water
- ½tablespoon oil
- ½ inch ginger, finely chopped
- 1tomato, chopped
- ½teaspoon salt

Directions:

1. Put the oil,garlic, ginger and cumin seeds in the Instant Pot and select "Sauté".
2. Sauté for 35 seconds and add tomato paste and salt.
3. Add the water and lentils, and mix well.
4. Set the instant pot to "Manual" and cook for 4 minutes at high pressure.
5. Release the pressure quickly and open the lid.
6. Add spinach and select "Sauté".
7. Sauté for 3 minutes and dish out.

Nutritional Information per Serving:

Calories: 147; Total Fat: 3.1g; Carbs: 23.1g; Sugars: 1.98g; Protein: 8.3g;

Cholesterol: 0mg; Sodium: 414mg

62.Confetti Rice

Yield: 4 Servings

Total Time: 17 Minutes

Prep Time: 5 Minutes

Cook Time: 12 Minutes

Ingredients

- 1 cup lengthy grain white rice
- 3 cups frozen peas, thawed
- 3 tablespoons butter
- 2 cloves garlic, minced
- 1 cup vegetable broth
- ¼ cup lemon juice
- 1 small onion, chopped
- 1 tablespoon cumin powder
- ½ teaspoon salt
- ½ teaspoon black pepper

Directions:

1. Put the butter and onions in the Instant Pot and select "Sauté".
2. Sauté for 3 minutes and add rest of the ingredients.
3. Set the instant pot to "Manual" and cook for 8 minutes at high pressure.
4. Release the pressure naturally and serve with some freshly grated coriander leaves.

Nutritional Information per Serving:
Calories: 333; Total Fat: 13.5g; Carbs: 40.6g; Sugars: 9.4g; Protein: 13.2g; Cholesterol: 31mg; Sodium: 627mg

63.Coconut Rice

Yield: 4 Servings

Total Time: 15 Minutes

Prep Time: 5 Minutes

Cook Time: 10 Minutes

Ingredients

- 1 cup unsweetened coconut, scraped or grated
- 1½ cup lengthy grain white rice
- 3 tablespoons butter
- 3 cups water
- ½ cup currants
- 1 teaspoon cinnamon powder
- ¼ teaspoon cloves
- ¾ teaspoon salt

Directions:

1. Put the butter and all the ingredients except rice and water in the Instant Pot and select "Sauté".
2. Sauté for 2 minutes and add rice and water.
3. Set the instant pot to "Manual" and cook for 6 minutes at high pressure.
4. Release the pressure naturally and dish out.

Nutritional Information per Serving:

Calories: 353; Total Fat: 26.9g; Carbs: 26.8g; Sugars: 3.1g; Protein: 3.7g; Cholesterol: 23mg; Sodium: 515mg

64.Bok Choy Rice

Yield: 5 Servings

Total Time: 22 Minutes

Prep Time: 10 Minutes

Cook Time: 12 Minutes

Ingredients

- 1½ cups rice
- 3 cups chopped bokchoy, leaves and stems trimmed
- 1 tablespoon olive oil
- ½ cup garlic, chopped
- ½ cup onions, chopped
- 3 cups hot vegetable broth
- ½ cup white wine
- ½ teaspoon red pepper flakes
- ½ teaspoon salt

Directions:

1. Put the olive oil, onions and garlic in the Instant Pot and select "Sauté".
2. Sauté for 4 minutes and add rice, vegetable broth and wine.
3. Set the instant pot to "Manual" and cook for 6 minutes at high pressure.
4. Release the pressure naturally and add bokchoy.
5. Let it simmer for 5 minutes.

Nutritional Information per Serving:
Calories: 286; Total Fat: 3.4g; Carbs: 53.4g; Sugars: 2.6g; Protein: 5.6g;

Cholesterol: 0mg; Sodium: 585mg

65.Saffron Cream Cheese Rice

Yield: 4 Servings

Total Time: 20 Minutes

Prep Time: 8 Minutes

Cook Time: 12 Minutes

Ingredients

- 2 cups rice
- 3 tablespoons olive oil
- 1 cup onions, finely chopped
- 1 teaspoon saffron threads, dissolved in warm water
- 3 garlic cloves, minced
- 1 cup white wine
- 4 cups hot vegetable broth
- 2 tablespoons fresh lemon juice
- 8 oz. soft cream cheese
- ½ cup pecans, coarsely chopped
- Salt and black pepper, to taste

Directions:

1. Put the olive oil, onions and garlic in the Instant Pot and select "Sauté".
2. Sauté for 4 minutes and add rest of the ingredients except soft cream cheese and lemon juice.
3. Set the instant pot to "Manual" and cook for 6 minutes at high pressure.
4. Release the pressure naturally and add lemon juice and softened cream cheese.

Nutritional Information per Serving:
Calories: 575; Total Fat: 25.8g; Carbs: 67.2g; Sugars: 3.3g; Protein: 9.3g;

Cholesterol: 50mg; Sodium: 567mg

66.Sunny Lentils

Yield: 4 Servings

Total Time: 25 Minutes

Prep Time: 10 Minutes

Cook Time: 15 Minutes

Ingredients

- 1 cup red lentils
- 1 tablespoon olive oil
- 1/3 cup green bell pepper, chopped
- 1 tablespoon garlic, minced
- 1/3 cup onions, chopped
- 1/3 cup red bell pepper, chopped
- ½ teaspoon dried tarragon
- 1 cup tomatoes, diced
- 3 tablespoons sweetened coconut, shredded
- ¼ teaspoon curry powder
- ½ cup water
- Salt and black pepper, to taste

Directions:

1. Put the olive oil, onions, garlic, green bell pepper, red bell pepper, tarragon and spices in the Instant Pot and select "Sauté".
2. Sauté for 5 minutes and add tomatoes, red lentils and coconut.
3. Set the instant pot to "Manual" and cook for 8 minutes at high pressure.
4. Release the pressure naturally and dish out..

Nutritional Information per Serving:
Calories: 235; Total Fat: 5.5g; Carbs: 34.4g; Sugars: 3.8g; Protein: 13.4g;

Cholesterol: 0mg; Sodium: 8mg

67.Coconut Red Lentil Curry

Yield: 6 Servings

Total Time: 35 Minutes

Prep Time: 5 Minutes

Cook Time: 30 Minutes

Ingredients

- 1 cup red kidney beans, soaked overnight
- 1½ cups black gram beans, soaked overnight
- 2 cups coconut cream
- 2 cups water
- 2 tablespoons oil
- 2 teaspoons cumin seeds
- 1 cup onions, finely diced
- ½ teaspoon turmeric powder
- 3 tablespoons fresh ginger, grated

- 3 cups tomatoes, diced
- ½ cup cilantro
- 3 teaspoons salt
- 3 teaspoons red chilli powder
- 2 teaspoons garam masala

Directions:

1. Put the oil,onions and cumin seeds in the Instant Pot and select "Sauté".
2. Sauté for 4 minutes and add tomatoes,turmeric powder, ginger, salt, red chilli powder and beans.
3. Sauté for 3 minutes and add water.
4. Set the instant pot to "Manual" mode for 18 minutes at high pressure.
5. Release the pressure naturally for 5 minutes and stir in coconut cream and garam masala.

Nutritional Information per Serving:
Calories: 422; Total Fat: 24.7g; Carbs: 41.3g; Sugars: 6.6g; Protein: 14g; Cholesterol: 0mg; Sodium: 1190mg

68.Kale Rice

Yield: 4 Servings

Total Time: 25 Minutes

Prep Time: 10 Minutes

Cook Time: 15 Minutes

Ingredients

- 1½ cups rice

- 1 bunch kale leaves, chopped and stems removed
- 2 tablespoons olive oil
- 1 cup onions, finely chopped
- 2 garlic cloves, minced
- ½ cup white wine
- 3½ cups vegetable stock
- 2 tablespoons basil, chopped
- ½ cup Parmesan, grated
- ½ teaspoon salt
- ½ teaspoon black pepper
- ½ teaspoon red pepper flakes
- 2 tablespoons apple cider vinegar

Directions:

1. Put the olive oil, onions and garlic in the Instant Pot and select "Sauté".
2. Sauté for 4 minutes and add rice, wine and vegetable broth.
3. Set the instant pot to "Manual" mode for 5 minutes at high pressure.
4. Release the pressure naturally and add kale leaves and chopped herbs.
5. Select "Sauté" and cook for 5 minutes.
6. Stir in the apple cider vinegar, salt, black pepper, cheese and red pepper flakes.
7. Mix well and serve hot.

Nutritional Information per Serving:
Calories: 304; Total Fat: 6.7g; Carbs: 50g; Sugars: 1.8g; Protein: 6g;
Cholesterol: 2mg; Sodium: 305mg

69.Walnut Cheese Rice

Yield: 5 Servings

Total Time: 15 Minutes

Prep Time: 5 Minutes

Cook Time: 10 Minutes

Ingredients

- 1½ cups rice
- 2 tablespoons olive oil
- 3½ cups vegetable stock
- 1 cup onions, finely chopped
- 2 garlic cloves, minced
- 2 tablespoons fresh lemon juice
- 3 oz. soft cream cheese
- 1 cup parmesan cheese
- 3 tablespoons blue cheese, crumbled
- ½ cup walnuts, coarsely chopped
- Salt and black pepper, to taste

Directions:

1. Put the olive oil,onions and garlic in the Instant Pot and select "Sauté".
2. Sauté for 4 minutes and add rice and vegetable broth.
3. Set the instant pot to "Manual" mode for 5 minutes at high pressure.
4. Release the pressure naturally and add lemon juice, salt, black pepper and all types of cheese.
5. Garnish with chopped walnuts and serve warm.

Nutritional Information per Serving:

Calories: 440; Total Fat: 22.1g; Carbs: 49.7g; Sugars: 1.9g; Protein: 11.8g;

Cholesterol: 27mg; Sodium: 213mg

70.Creamy Mushroom Alfredo Rice

Yield: 4 Servings

Total Time: 15 Minutes

Prep Time: 5 Minutes

Cook Time: 10 Minutes

Ingredients

- 1 cup rice
- 2 tablespoons olive oil
- 2¾ cups vegetable stock
- ¾ cup onions, finely chopped
- 2 garlic cloves, minced
- 1½ tablespoons fresh lemon juice
- 2 oz. Bertolli creamy mushroom Alfredo sauce
- Salt and black pepper, to taste
- ¼ cup walnuts, coarsely chopped

Directions:

1. Put the olive oil,onions and garlic in the Instant Pot and select "Sauté".
2. Sauté for 3 minutes and add rice and vegetable broth.
3. Set the instant pot to "Manual" mode for 5 minutes at high pressure.

4. Release the pressure naturally and add lemon juice, salt, black pepper and Bertolli creamy mushroom Alfredo sauce.

5. Garnish with chopped walnuts and serve warm.

Nutritional Information per Serving:
Calories: 332; Total Fat: 15.4g; Carbs: 42.1g; Sugars: 2.3g; Protein: 7g; Cholesterol: 11; Sodium: 117 mg

Innovative Egg Recipes

71.Eggs De Provence

Yield: 3 Servings

Total Time: 30 Minutes

Prep Time: 10 Minutes

Cook Time: 20 Minutes

Ingredients

- 3 eggs
- ½ cup meatless bacon
- ½ cup kale leaves, chopped
- ¾ teaspoon Herbed Provence
- ¼ cup onions, chopped
- ½ cup heavy cream
- ½ cup cheddar cheese
- Salt and black pepper, to taste

Directions

1.Whisk eggs and heavy cream, and then add the remaining ingredients.

2.Beat well and transfer the mixture into a heat proof dish.

3.Place the trivet inside the Instant Pot.

4.Set the instant pot to "Manual" mode for 18 minutes at high pressure.

5.Release the pressure naturally and dish out.

Nutritional Information per Serving:

Calories: 340; Total Fat: 27.5g; Carbs: 3.6g; Sugars: 0.9g; Protein: 19.4g; Cholesterol: 234mg; Sodium: 687mg

72.Devilled Scotch Eggs

Yield: 6 Servings

Total Time: 22 Minutes

Prep Time: 10 Minutes

Cook Time: 12 Minutes

Ingredients

- 6 large eggs
- 1½ tablespoons oil
- 1½ pounds meatless bacon slices
- 6 tablespoons Greek yogurt
- 3 teaspoons mustard sauce
- 6 tablespoons mayonnaise
- Italian seasoning, for garnish
- Water, as per required

Directions:

1. Place the trivet inside the Instant Pot and add eggs and water.
2. Set the instant pot to "Manual" mode for 6 minutes at high pressure.
3. Release the pressure naturally and transfer the eggs into ice cold water.
4. Remove the shells and fold the bacon slices gently around the eggs.
5. Put the oil and scotch eggs in the Instant Pot and select "Sauté".

6. Sauté for 3 minutes and place the trivet inside the Instant Pot.

7. Put the eggs and water and lock the lid.

8. Set the instant pot to "Manual" mode for 5 minutes at high pressure.

9. Release the pressure quickly and dish out.

10. Scoop out the yolks and mix rest of the ingredients.

11. Put inside the hollow eggs and garnish with Italian seasoning.

Nutritional Information per Serving:
Calories: 288; Total Fat: 23.7g; Carbs: 8.9g; Sugars: 4.8g; Protein: 12g;

Cholesterol: 213mg; Sodium: 192mg

73.Egg Spinach Quiche

Yield: 6 Servings

Total Time: 35 Minutes

Prep Time: 15 Minutes

Cook Time: 20 Minutes

Ingredients

- 6 large eggs
- ¼ cup milk
- ¼ teaspoon salt
- ¼ teaspoon black pepper
- 1½ cups fresh baby spinach, roughly chopped
- ½ cup mushrooms, chopped
- 2 green onions, sliced
- 2 mushroom slices, topping the quiche

- ¼ cup parmesan cheese, shredded

Directions:

1. Mix eggs, salt, black pepper and milk in a bowl.

2. Put the mushrooms, baby spinach and mushrooms in a baking quiche mould.

3. Top with the egg mixture, mushroom slices and parmesan cheese.

4. Place the trivet inside the Instant Pot and add water and quiche mold.

5. Set the instant pot to "Manual" mode for 18 minutes at high pressure.

6. Release the pressure naturally and serve hot.

Nutritional Information per Serving:

Calories: 90; Total Fat: 5.6g; Carbs: 2.6g; Sugars: 1.2g; Protein: 8.1g; Cholesterol: 188mg; Sodium: 205mg

74.Egg Muffins

Yield: 4 Servings

Total Time: 20 Minutes

Prep Time: 10 Minutes

Cook Time: 10 Minutes

Ingredients

- 4 eggs
- 4 slices meatless bacon, precooked
- 1 green onion, diced
- ¼ teaspoon lemon pepper seasoning
- ¼ cup cheddar cheese, shredded

Directions:

1. Whisk the eggs with all other ingredients and divide the muffin batter equally in muffin moulds.

2. Place the trivet inside the Instant Pot and add water.

3. Put the muffin molds on the trivet.

4. Set the instant pot to "Manual" mode for 8 minutes at high pressure.

5. Release the pressure naturally and serve hot.

Nutritional Information per Serving:

Calories: 196; Total Fat: 14.7g; Carbs: 1.1g; Sugars: 0.5g; Protein: 14.4g; Cholesterol: 192mg; Sodium: 545mg

75.Zesty Eggs

Yield: 4 Servings

Total Time: 18 Minutes

Prep Time: 10 Minutes

Cook Time: 8 Minutes

Ingredients

- 4 eggs
- 1½ tablespoons Greek yogurt
- 1½ tablespoons mayonnaise
- 1 teaspoon jalapeno mustard
- ¼ teaspoon onion powder
- ¼ teaspoon paprika
- ¼ teaspoon lemon zests

- Salt and black pepper, to taste

Directions:

1. Place the trivet inside the Instant Pot and add eggs and water.

2. Set the instant pot to "Manual" mode for 6 minutes at high pressure.

3. Release the pressure naturally and transfer the eggs into ice cold water.

4. Scoop out the egg yolks and mix with rest of the ingredients.

5. Fill the hollow eggs with this mixture and serve.

Nutritional Information per Serving:
Calories: 88; Total Fat: 6.3g; Carbs: 2g; Sugars: 0.8g; Protein: 5.8g;

Cholesterol: 165mg; Sodium: 123mg

76.Cheesy Spinach Eggs

Yield: 2 Servings

Total Time: 15 Minutes

Prep Time: 10 Minutes

Cook Time: 5 Minutes

Ingredients

- 3 eggs

- 5 cups fresh baby spinach

- 2 tablespoons water

- 2 tablespoons feta cheese, crumbled

- Salt and black pepper, to taste

Directions:

1. Put the spinach, salt, black pepper and eggs in the Instant Pot.

2. Set the instant pot to "Manual" mode for 3 minutes at high pressure.

3. Release the pressure naturally and place the trivet in the Instant Pot.

4. Put the spinach in a baking dish, crack eggs over it and sprinkle feta cheese.

5. Set the instant pot to "Manual" mode for 5 minutes at high pressure.

6. Release the pressure naturally and dish out.

Nutritional Information per Serving:
Calories: 91; Total Fat: 5.9g; Carbs: 2.4g; Sugars: 0.8g; Protein: 7.9g;

Cholesterol: 169mg; Sodium: 171mg

77.Egg Custard

Yield: 8 Servings

Total Time: 45 Minutes

Prep Time: 10 Minutes

Cook Time: 35 Minutes

Ingredients

- 6 eggs

- 24-ounce milk

- ½ cup honey

- ¼ teaspoon ground cinnamon

- ¼ teaspoon ground cardamom

- 1/8 teaspoon ground allspice

- ¼ teaspoon ground ginger

- ¼ teaspoon ground nutmeg

- 1/8 teaspoon ground cloves

- Salt, to taste

Directions:

1. Whisk eggs with all other ingredients and divide evenly into 8 small ramekins.

2. Place the trivet inside the Instant Pot and arrange ramekins in it.

3. Set the instant pot to "Manual" mode for 30 minutes at low pressure.

4. Release the pressure naturally and keep aside to cool.

Nutritional Information per Serving:
Calories: 155; Total Fat: 5.1g; Carbs: 22.1g; Sugars: 21.5g; Protein: 7g; Cholesterol: 130mg; Sodium: 87mg

78.Cobb-Style Egg Potato

Yield: 6 Servings

Total Time: 18 Minutes

Prep Time: 10 Minutes

Cook Time: 8 Minutes

Ingredients

- 6 hard-boiled eggs
- 2 medium potatoes, sliced
- 1 avocado, cubed
- 3 meatless bacon slices, cooked and crumbled

Directions:

1. Boil the eggs in the Instant Pot and slice lengthwise.

2. Put the potato slices in the Instant Pot and lock the lid.

3. Set the instant pot to "Manual" mode for 7 minutes at high pressure.

4. Release the pressure naturally and dish out.

5. Top each with an egg slice and add cubed avocado on the top.

6. Divide bacon crumbles evenly and serve.

Nutritional Information per Serving:
Calories: 188; Total Fat: 11.7g; Carbs: 14.5g; Sugars: 1.3g; Protein: 7.6g;

Cholesterol: 164mg; Sodium: 105mg

79.Egg Zucchini

Yield: 2 Servings

Total Time: 15 Minutes

Prep Time: 10 Minutes

Cook Time: 5 Minutes

Ingredients

- 1 zucchini, cut into ½ inch round slices

- ½ teaspoon dried dill

- ½ teaspoon paprika

- 1 egg

- 1 tablespoon coconut oil

- 1½ tablespoons coconut flour

- 1 tablespoon milk

- Salt and black pepper, to taste

Directions:

1.Whisk egg and almond milk together in a small bowl.

2.Mix the salt, black pepper, paprika, dried dill and coconut flour in another bowl.

3.Dip the zucchini slices in the egg mixture and then in the dry mixture.

4.Put the coconut oil in the Instant Pot and add the zucchini slices.

5.Set the instant pot to "Manual" mode for 4 minutes at high pressure.

6.Release the pressure naturally and dish out.

Nutritional Information per Serving:
Calories: 134; Total Fat: 10g; Carbs: 8g; Sugars: 2.3g; Protein: 5.1g; Cholesterol: 82mg; Sodium: 45mg

80.Mini Egg Frittatas

Yield: 4 Servings

Total Time: 18 Minutes

Prep Time: 10 Minutes

Cook Time: 8 Minutes

Ingredients

5 eggs

4 cooked meatless bacon slices, crumbled

½ cup milk

1 green onion, chopped

¼ teaspoon lemon pepper seasoning

4 tablespoons cheddar cheese, shredded

Salt and black pepper, to taste

Directions:

1. Place the trivet in the bottom of Instant Pot and add water.

2. Beat together milk, eggs, lemon pepper seasoning, salt and black pepper in a bowl.

3. Add remaining ingredients and stir to combine.

4. Transfer the mixture into small molds and place the molds on the trivet.

5. Place the molds on top of trivet.

6. Set the instant pot to "Manual" mode for 6 minutes at high pressure.

7. Release the pressure quickly and dish out.

Nutritional Information per Serving:
Calories: 227; Total Fat: 16.4g; Carbs: 2.6g; Sugars: 1.9g; Protein: 16.8g; Cholesterol: 235mg; Sodium: 575mg

81.Egg and Scallion Omelette

Yield: 2 Servings

Total Time: 15 Minutes

Prep Time: 10 Minutes

Cook Time: 5 Minutes

Ingredients

- 2 eggs
- 2 small scallions, chopped
- ¼ teaspoon garlic powder
- ¼ teaspoon sesame seeds
- ½ cup water
- Salt and black pepper, to taste

Directions:

1. Place the trivet in the bottom of Instant Pot and add water.

2. Beat together water, garlic powder, salt and black pepper with eggs.

3. Stir in the scallion and sesame seeds.

4. Transfer the bowl on the trivet.

5. Set the instant pot to "Manual" mode for 5 minutes at high pressure.

6. Release the pressure quickly and dish out.

Nutritional Information per Serving:
Calories: 68; Total Fat: 4.6g; Carbs: 1.1g; Sugars: 0.6g; Protein: 5.8g;

Cholesterol: 164mg; Sodium: 64mg

82.Egg and Bacon Casserole

Yield: 6 Servings

Total Time: 20 Minutes

Prep Time: 10 Minutes

Cook Time: 10 Minutes

Ingredients

- 6 eggs

- ½ pound meatless bacon, cooked and chopped

- 1 tablespoon coconut oil

- 1 small green bell pepper, seeded and chopped

- 1 large sweet potatoes, peeled and grated

- ½ cup coconut milk

- ½ teaspoon dried dill, crushed

- 1 small onion, chopped

- 1 garlic clove, minced
- Pinch of red pepper flakes, crushed
- Salt and freshly ground black pepper, to taste

Directions:

1. Beat together coconut milk, eggs, salt and black pepper in a bowl.
2. Put the oil, garlic, onions and green bell peppers in the Instant Pot and select "Sauté".
3. Sauté for 5 minutes and add sweet potato and red pepper flakes.
4. Sauté for 3 minutes and add rest of the ingredients and top with the egg mixture.
5. Set the instant pot to "Manual" and cook for 8 minutes at high pressure.
6. Release the pressure quickly and cut into equal sized wedges to serve.

Nutritional Information per Serving:
Calories: 203; Total Fat: 14.6g; Carbs: 11.9g; Sugars: 2.6g; Protein: 7.9g; Cholesterol: 164mg; Sodium: 223mg

83.Egg Veggie Pie

Yield: 8 Servings

Total Time: 20 Minutes

Prep Time: 10 Minutes

Cook Time: 10 Minutes

Ingredients

- 16 eggs, beaten
- 2 sweet potatoes, peeled and shredded

- 2 red bell peppers, seeded and chopped
- 2 onions, chopped
- 2 garlic cloves, minced
- 4 teaspoons fresh basil, chopped
- Salt and black pepper, to taste

Directions:

1. Put all the ingredients in the Instant Pot and mix well.
2. Set the instant pot to "Manual" and cook for 8 minutes at high pressure.
3. Release the pressure naturally and dish out.

Nutritional Information per Serving:

Calories: 192; Total Fat: 8.9g; Carbs: 16.2g; Sugars: 3.6g; Protein: 12.3g; Cholesterol: 327mg; Sodium: 129mg

84.Egg Avocado Boats

Yield: 4 Servings

Total Time: 20 Minutes

Prep Time: 10 Minutes

Cook Time: 10 Minutes

Ingredients

- 4 eggs
- 3 slices meatless bacon
- 2 avocados, pitted and halved
- Freshly chopped chives, to garnish
- Salt and black pepper, to taste

Directions:

1. Crack the eggs inside the avocado halves.

2. Season with salt and pepper and place the avocados on the trivet.

3. Set the instant pot to "Manual" and cook for 8 minutes at high pressure.

4. Release the pressure naturally and top with bacon and chives.

Nutritional Information per Serving:

Calories: 280; Total Fat: 25.1g; Carbs: 9.3g; Sugars: 0.9g; Protein: 7.9g;

Cholesterol: 164mg; Sodium: 123mg

85.Egg and Bacon Cups

Yield: 6 Servings

Total Time: 25 Minutes

Prep Time: 10 Minutes

Cook Time: 15 Minutes

Ingredients

- 6 eggs

- 6 meatless bacon slices, cooked

- 1 tablespoon chives, chopped

- Salt and black pepper, to taste

Directions:

1. Put each bacon slice in each muffin tin wrapping around the outer edge.

2. Crack the eggs in each tin and top with chopped chives, salt and pepper.

3. Arrange the trivet in the Instant Pot and place the muffin tins on it.

4. Set the instant pot to "Manual" and cook for 12 minutes at high pressure.

5. Release the pressure naturally and serve hot.

Nutritional Information per Serving:
Calories: 79; Total Fat: 5.9g; Carbs: 0.7g; Sugars: 0.4g; Protein: 6.1g;

Cholesterol: 164mg; Sodium: 135mg

86.Quick Scrambled Eggs

Yield: 1 Serving

Total Time: 15 Minutes

Prep Time: 10 Minutes

Cook Time: 5 Minutes

Ingredients

- 2 eggs
- 1 tablespoon milk
- 1 tablespoon butter
- 1 cup water.
- Salt and black pepper, to taste

Directions:

1. Break the eggs in the bowl and add milk, salt and black pepper.
2. Beat gently and add the butter
3. Put water in the Instant pot and arrange the trivet.
4. Put the bowl on the trivet and close the lid.
5. Set the instant pot to "Manual" and cook for 6 minutes at low pressure.
6. Release the pressure quickly and serve hot.

Nutritional Information per Serving:

Calories: 235; Total Fat: 20.6g; Carbs: 1.4g; Sugars: 1.4g; Protein: 11.7g; Cholesterol: 359mg; Sodium: 219mg

87.Cheese and Tomatoes Egg Frittata

Yield: 4 Servings

Total Time: 15 Minutes

Prep Time: 10 Minutes

Cook Time: 5 Minutes

Ingredients

- 6 large eggs
- ½ cup cherry tomatoes, halved
- ½ cup feta, crumbled
- 2 tablespoons basil
- ½ onion, sliced
- 1 tablespoons ghee
- Salt and black pepper, to taste

Directions:

1. Break the eggs into a bowl and season with salt, pepper and basil.
2. Put the ghee and onions in the Instant Pot and select "Sauté".
3. Sauté for 4 minutes and add the egg mixture, feta cheese and cherry tomatoes.
4. Set the instant pot to "Manual" and cook for 2 minutes at low pressure.
5. Release the pressure naturally and serve warm.

Nutritional Information per Serving:

Calories: 195; Total Fat: 14.7g; Carbs: 3.6g; Sugars: 2.5g; Protein: 12.g; Cholesterol: 304mg; Sodium: 316mg

88.Turmeric Egg Potatoes

Yield: 3 Servings

Total Time: 20 Minutes

Prep Time: 10 Minutes

Cook Time: 10 Minutes

Ingredients

- 2 eggs, whisked
- 1 teaspoon ground turmeric
- 1 teaspoon cumin seeds
- 2 tablespoons olive oil
- 2 potatoes, peeled and diced
- 1 onion, finely chopped
- 2 teaspoons ginger-garlic paste
- ½ teaspoon red chilli powder
- Salt and black pepper, to taste

Directions:

1. Put the olive oil, cumin seeds, ginger-garlic paste and onions in the Instant Pot and select "Sauté".
2. Sauté for 4 minutes and add potatoes and rest of the ingredients.
3. Set the instant pot to "Manual" and cook for 6 minutes at high pressure.
4. Release the pressure naturally and serve warm.

Nutritional Information per Serving:
Calories: 265; Total Fat: 14.7g; Carbs: 28.1g; Sugars: 3.5g; Protein: 6.9g;

Cholesterol: 109mg; Sodium: 53mg

89.Egg and Garlic Skillet

Yield: 2 Servings

Total Time: 13 Minutes

Prep Time: 5 Minutes

Cook Time: 8 Minutes

Ingredients

- 2 eggs, whisked
- 1 tablespoon olive oil
- 2tomatoes, cut into 4 halves
- 2 teaspoons garlic, minced
- 1 green onion, chopped
- Salt and black pepper, to taste

Directions:

1. Put the olive oil, garlic and green onions in the Instant Pot and select "Sauté".
2. Sauté for 4 minutes and add tomatoes and eggs.
3. Set the instant pot to "Manual" and cook for 3 minutes at high pressure.
4. Release the pressure naturally and serve warm.

Nutritional Information per Serving:
Calories: 152; Total Fat: 11.6g; Carbs: 6.6g; Sugars: 3.8g; Protein: 6.9g;

Cholesterol: 164mg; Sodium: 69mg

90.Egg Pancakes

Yield: 5 Servings

Total Time: 35 Minutes

Prep Time: 10 Minutes

Cook Time: 25 Minutes

Ingredients

- 3 eggs
- 2 tablespoons honey
- ½ teaspoon ginger powder
- ½ cup milk
- 4 tablespoons lemon curd
- 1 cup self-rising flour
- 1 tablespoon baking powder
- 1 tablespoon butter, melted
- 3 mango slices

Directions:

1. Mix together self-rising flour, baking powder and ginger powder in a bowl.
2. Put the eggs, milk, honey and butter in it and mix well.
3. Put 2 tablespoons in the baking dish.
4. Place the trivet in the Instant Pot and put the baking dish in it.
5. Set the instant pot to "Manual" and cook for 5 minutes at low pressure.
6. Release the pressure naturally and repeat the process with the remaining mixture.
7. Stack all the pancakes into a plate and top with lemon curd and mango slices.

Nutritional Information per Serving:

Calories: 242; Total Fat: 10.5g; Carbs: 33g; Sugars: 12.3g; Protein: 7.6g;

Cholesterol: 146mg; Sodium: 108mg

Tasty Snacks Recipes

91.piced Nuts

Yield: 6 Servings

Total Time: 30 Minutes

Prep Time: 10 Minutes

Cook Time: 20 Minutes

Ingredients

- 1 cup cashews
- 1 cup almonds
- 1 cup pecans
- 1 cup raisins
- 1 tablespoon butter
- ½ teaspoon brown sugar
- ½ teaspoon black pepper
- 1½ teaspoon chilli powder
- ½ teaspoon sea salt
- ½ teaspoon garlic powder
- ¼ teaspoon cayenne pepper
- ½ teaspoon cumin powder

Directions:

1. Put the butter, almonds, cashews, raisins and pecans in the Instant Pot.
2. Season with all the spices and stir gently.
3. Set the instant pot to "Manual" and cook for 20 minutes at high pressure.

4. Release the pressure naturally and serve.

Nutritional Information per Serving:
Calories: 335; Total Fat: 22.4g; Carbs: 31.5g; Sugars: 16.5g; Protein: 8.1g;
Cholesterol: 5mg; Sodium: 177mg

92.Mushroom Spinach Treat

Yield: 3 Servings

Total Time: 22 Minutes

Prep Time: 10 Minutes

Cook Time: 12 Minutes

Ingredients

- ½ cup spinach
- ½ pound fresh mushrooms, sliced
- 2 garlic cloves, minced
- ½ cup chicken broth
- 2 tablespoons fresh thyme, chopped
- 1 onion, chopped
- 1 tablespoon olive oil
- 1 tablespoon fresh cilantro, chopped
- Salt and black pepper, to taste

Directions:

1. Put the olive oil, garlic and onions in the Instant Pot and select "Sauté".
2. Sauté for 4 minutes and add spinach, mushrooms, chicken broth, salt, black pepper and thyme.

3. Set the instant pot to "Manual" and cook for 7 minutes at high pressure.

4. Release the pressure naturally and garnish with cilantro.

Nutritional Information per Serving:
Calories: 86; Total Fat: 5.32g; Carbs: 8.1g; Sugars: 3g; Protein: 4g; Cholesterol: 0mg; Sodium: 138mg

93.Spicy Roasted Olives

Yield: 4 Servings

Total Time: 17 Minutes

Prep Time: 10 Minutes

Cook Time: 7 Minutes

Ingredients

- 2 cups green and black olives, mixed
- 2 tangerines
- 2 garlic cloves, minced
- 2 tablespoons vinegar
- ½ inch piece of turmeric, finely grated
- 1 fresh red chilli, thinly sliced
- 2 sprigs rosemary
- 1 tablespoon olive oil

Directions:

1.Put all the ingredients except the tangerines in the Instant Pot.

2.Squeeze the tangerines in the Instant Pot over all the ingredients.

3.Set the instant pot to "Manual" and cook for 6 minutes at high pressure.

4.Release the pressure naturally and dish out.

Nutritional Information per Serving:
Calories: 163; Total Fat: 13.6g; Carbs: 2.3g; Sugars: 0.5g; Protein: 0.4g;

Cholesterol: 0mg; Sodium: 561mg

94.Cooked Guacamole

Yield: 4 Servings

Total Time: 20 Minutes

Prep Time: 10 Minutes

Cook Time: 10 Minutes

Ingredients

- 1 large onion, finely diced

- 4 tablespoons lemon juice

- ¼ cup cilantro, chopped

- 4 avocados, peeled and diced

- 3 tablespoons olive oil

- 3 jalapenos, finely diced

- Salt and black pepper, to taste

Directions:

1. Put the olive oil and onions in the Instant Pot and select "Sauté".

2. Sauté for 3 minutes and add cilantro, lemon juice, avocados, salt, black pepper and jalapenos.

3. Set the instant pot to "Manual" and cook for 6 minutes at high pressure.

4. Release the pressure naturally and dish out.

Nutritional Information per Serving:
Calories: 401; Total Fat: 37.4g; Carbs: 19.4g; Sugars: 2.8g; Protein: 4.18g;

Cholesterol: 0mg; Sodium: 19mg

95.Butternut Squash

Yield: 2 Servings

Total Time: 17 Minutes

Prep Time: 10 Minutes

Cook Time: 7 Minutes

Ingredients

- 1 whole butternut squash, washed
- 1 tablespoon butter
- 1 tablespoon BBQ sauce
- Salt and black pepper, to taste
- ¼ teaspoon smoked paprika

Directions:

1. Season the butternut squash with paprika, salt and pepper.
2. Put the butter and seasoned whole butternut squash in the Instant Pot.
3. Set the instant pot to "Manual" and cook for 6 minutes at high pressure.
4. Release the pressure naturally and top with BBQ sauce.

Nutritional Information per Serving:
Calories: 154; Total Fat: 6.6g; Carbs: 19.5g; Sugars: 5.6g; Protein: 3.1g;

Cholesterol: 15mg; Sodium: 318mg

96.Baked Potato

Yield: 2 Servings

Total Time: 40 Minutes

Prep Time: 10 Minutes

Cook Time: 30 Minutes

Ingredients

- 2medium potatoes, well-scrubbed
- 1 tablespoon olive oil
- 2 sheets aluminium foil
- ¼ cup sour cream
- Salt, to taste

Directions:

1. Arrange the trivet in the Instant Pot.
2. Rub the potatoes with olive oil and salt.
3. Wrap the potatoes tightly in the aluminium foil.
4. Transfer the potatoes on the trivet.
5. Set the instant pot to "Manual" and cook for 30 minutes at low pressure.
6. Release the pressure naturally and fill in the sour cream.

Nutritional Information per Serving:

Calories: 269; Total Fat: 13.2g; Carbs: 34.7g; Sugars: 2.5g; Protein: 4.5g;

Cholesterol: 13mg; Sodium: 28mg

97.Cajun Spiced Pecans

Yield: 3 Servings

Total Time: 30 Minutes

Prep Time: 10 Minutes

Cook Time: 20 Minutes

Ingredients

- ½ pound pecan halves
- 1 teaspoon dried basil
- 1 teaspoon dried thyme
- ½ tablespoon chilli powder
- ¼ teaspoon garlic powder
- ¼ teaspoon cayenne pepper
- 1 tablespoon olive oil
- 1 teaspoon dried oregano
- Salt, to taste

Directions:

1.Put all the ingredients in the Instant Pot.

2.Set the instant pot to "Manual" and cook for 20 minutes at low pressure.

3.Release the pressure naturally and serve.

Nutritional Information per Serving:

Calories: 345; Total Fat: 33.1g; Carbs: 7.2g; Sugars: 0.1g; Protein: 4.4g; Cholesterol: 0mg; Sodium: 0mg

98.Creamy Cheese Avocado

Yield: 3 Servings

Total Time: 15 Minutes

Prep Time: 10 Minutes

Cook Time: 5 Minutes

Ingredients

- 3 avocados, peeled, pitted and chopped
- ½ cup cream cheese, softened
- 3 garlic cloves, minced
- 3 tablespoon of fresh lemon juice
- Salt and black pepper, to taste

Directions:

1. Season the avocados with salt and black pepper.
2. Put the seasoned avocados and garlic cloves in the Instant Pot.
3. Set the instant pot to "Manual" and cook for 3 minutes at high pressure.
4. Release the pressure naturally and dish out the avocados.
5. Stir in lemon juice and cream cheese to the avocados.
6. Refrigerate before serving.

Nutritional Information per Serving:
Calories: 265; Total Fat: 23.8g; Carbs: 10.3g; Sugars: 2.9g; Protein: 5.5g;

Cholesterol: 43mg; Sodium: 120mg

99.Portobello Mushroom Burger

Yield: 3 Servings

Total Time: 15 Minutes

Prep Time: 30 Minutes

Cook Time: 10 Minutes

Ingredients

- 3 Portobello mushroom caps
- 1 tablespoon garlic, minced
- 1 teaspoon dried oregano, crushed
- 1 teaspoon dried basil, crushed
- ¼ cup balsamic vinegar
- 2 tablespoons olive oil
- 3 (1-ounce) Parmesan cheese slices
- Salt and black pepper, to taste

Directions:

1. Mix together all the ingredients except cheese slices and mushroom caps.
2. Arrange the mushroom caps smooth side up in a baking dish.
3. Top evenly with herb mixture and keep aside for 20 minutes.
4. Place the trivet in the Instant Pot and put the baking dish on it.
5. Set the instant pot to "Manual" and cook for 8 minutes at high pressure.
6. Release the pressure naturally and top with 1 cheese slice each.

Nutritional Information per Serving:

Calories: 187; Total Fat: 15.5g; Carbs: 3.9g; Sugars: 0.6g; Protein: 10g;

Cholesterol: 20mg; Sodium: 263mg

100.Energy Booster Cookies

Yield: 6 Servings

Total Time: 20 Minutes

Prep Time: 10 Minutes

Cook Time: 10 Minutes

Ingredients

- 2 large eggs
- 2/3 cup cocoa powder
- 1/3 cup sugar
- 1¼ cups almond butter
- Salt, to taste

Directions:

1. Put all the ingredients in a food processor and pulse.
2. Roll the mixture into 12 equal small balls and press them.
3. Arrange the balls onto a cookie sheet in a single layer.
4. Place the trivet in the Instant Pot and transfer the cookie sheet on it.
5. Set the instant pot to "Manual" and cook for 10 minutes at high pressure.
6. Release the pressure naturally and dish out the cookies.

Nutritional Information per Serving:

Calories: 107; Total Fat: 4.8g; Carbs: 17.1g; Sugars: 11.6g; Protein: 4.5g; Cholesterol: 62mg; Sodium: 25mg

101.Cheese Biscuits

Yield: 4 Servings

Total Time: 20 Minutes

Prep Time: 10 Minutes

Cook Time: 10 Minutes

Ingredients

- ½ cup coconut flour, sifted
- ¼ cup butter, melted and cooled
- ¼ tablespoon baking powder
- 1 teaspoon garlic powder
- 5 eggs
- 1 cup cheddar cheese, shredded
- Salt, to taste

Directions:

1. Mix together garlic powder, baking powder, coconut flour and salt in a bowl.
2. Beat eggs with butter in another bowl and mix with the flour mixture.
3. Add the cheese and place the mixture onto prepared cookie sheets with a tablespoon.
4. Place the trivet in the Instant Pot and transfer the cookie sheet on it.
5. Set the instant pot to "Manual" and cook for 10 minutes at high pressure.
6. Release the pressure naturally and dish out the biscuits.

Nutritional Information per Serving:

Calories: 357; Total Fat: 27.9g; Carbs: 11.7g; Sugars: 0.8g; Protein: 16.2g; Cholesterol: 265mg; Sodium: 335mg

102.Zucchini Sticks

Yield: 8 Servings

Total Time: 15 Minutes

Prep Time: 10 Minutes

Cook Time: 5 Minutes

Ingredients

- 3 zucchini, cut into 3-inch sticks lengthwise
- 3 eggs
- ¾ cup almonds, grounded
- ¾ cup Parmesan cheese, grated
- ¾ teaspoon Italian herb seasoning
- Salt and black pepper, to taste

Directions:

1. Season zucchini sticks with salt and black pepper.
2. Beat the eggs and mix together remaining ingredients.
3. Dip the zucchini sticks in egg and then coat with the cheese mixture.
4. Put the zucchini sticks onto prepared baking sheet.
5. Place the trivet in the Instant Pot and transfer the cookie sheet on it.
6. Set the instant pot to "Manual" and cook for 20 minutes at high pressure.
7. Release the pressure naturally and dish out.

Nutritional Information per Serving:

Calories: 127; Total Fat: 9.1g; Carbs: 6.1g; Sugars: 2.4g; Protein: 7.6g;

Cholesterol: 84mg; Sodium: 74mg

103.Grilled Peaches

Yield: 5 Servings

Total Time: 15 Minutes

Prep Time: 7 Minutes

Cook Time: 8 Minutes

Ingredients

- 5 medium peaches
- ¼ teaspoon ground cloves
- ½ teaspoon ground cinnamon
- ½ teaspoon brown sugar
- 2 tablespoons olive oil
- ¼ teaspoon salt

Directions

1. Remove the pits from the peaches and add olive oil on the cut side of the peaches.
2. Sprinkle the peaches with salt, cloves, cinnamon and brown sugar.
3. Place the trivet in the Instant Pot and transfer the peaches on it.
4. Set the instant pot to "Manual" and cook for 7 minutes at high pressure.
5. Release the pressure naturally and dish out.

Nutritional Information per Serving:

Calories: 109; Total Fat: 6g; Carbs: 14.6g; Sugars: 14.3g; Protein: 1.4g; Cholesterol: 0mg; Sodium: 0mg

104.Honey Citrus Roasted Cashews

Yield: 2 Servings

Total Time: 35 Minutes

Prep Time: 10 Minutes

Cook Time: 25 Minutes

Ingredients

- ¾ cup cashews
- ¼ teaspoon salt
- ¼ teaspoon ginger powder
- 1 teaspoon orange zest, minced
- 4 tablespoons honey

Directions

1. Mix together honey, orange zest, ginger powder and salt.
2. Add cashews to this mixture and place it in a ramekin.
3. Place the trivet in the Instant Pot and transfer the cashews on it.
4. Set the instant pot to "Manual" and cook for 20 minutes at high pressure.
5. Release the pressure naturally and dish out.

Nutritional Information per Serving:
Calories: 292; Total Fat: 12.3g; Carbs: 43g; Sugars: 34.5g; Protein: 5.2g;

Cholesterol: 0mg; Sodium: 295mg

105.Pumpkin Muffins

Yield: 10 Servings

Total Time: 25 Minutes

Prep Time: 10 Minutes

Cook Time: 15 Minutes

Ingredients

- 2 cups almond flour
- 4 tablespoons coconut flour
- 1½ teaspoons baking soda
- 2 teaspoons pumpkin pie spice
- ¼ teaspoon salt
- 1 cup pumpkin puree
- 3 teaspoons almond butter
- 1½ teaspoons baking powder
- ½ teaspoon ground cinnamon
- 3 large eggs
- ½ cup raw honey
- 2 tablespoon almonds, toasted and chopped

Directions:

1. Whisk together almond flour, coconut flour, cinnamon, baking soda, baking powder, salt and pumpkin pie spice.
2. Whisk together eggs, honey, pumpkin puree and butter.
3. Combine both the wet and dry mixtures.
4. Fill inside the muffin cups and top with almonds.
5. Place the trivet in the Instant Pot and transfer the muffin cups on it.
6. Set the instant pot to "Manual" and cook for 12 minutes at high pressure.
7. Release the pressure naturally and dish out.

Nutritional Information per Serving:

Calories: 268; Total Fat: 15.9g; Carbs: 25.7g; Sugars: 15.1g; Protein: 8.7g; Cholesterol: 56mg; Sodium: 784mg

106.Banana Chips

Yield: 3 Servings

Total Time: 40 Minutes

Prep Time: 10 Minutes

Cook Time: 30 Minutes

Ingredients

- 3 bananas, cut into 1/8 inch slices
- 3 tablespoons lemon juice
- 3 tablespoons nutmeg

Directions

1. Mix together all the ingredients in a bowl.
2. Spread banana slices evenly over baking sheet in one layer.
3. Place the trivet in the Instant Pot and transfer the baking sheet on it.
4. Set the instant pot to "Manual" and cook for 25 minutes at high pressure.
5. Release the pressure naturally and dish out.

Nutritional Information per Serving:

Calories: 145; Total Fat: 3.1g; Carbs: 30.7g; Sugars: 16.7g; Protein: 1.8g; Cholesterol: 0mg; Sodium: 5mg

107.Mustard Flavoured Artichokes

Yield: 3 Servings

Total Time: 25 Minutes

Prep Time: 10 Minutes

Cook Time: 15 Minutes

Ingredients

- 3 artichokes
- 3 tablespoons mayonnaise
- 1 cup water
- 2 pinches paprika
- 2 lemons, sliced in half
- 2 teaspoons Dijon mustard

Directions:

1. Mix together mayonnaise, paprika and Dijon mustard.
2. Place the trivet in the Instant Pot and add water.
3. Put the artichokes upwards and arrange lemon slices on it.
4. Set the instant pot to "Manual" and cook for 12 minutes at high pressure.
5. Release the pressure naturally and put the artichokes in the mayonnaise mixture.

Nutritional Information per Serving:

Calories: 147; Total Fat: 5.4g; Carbs: 24.4g; Sugars: 3.6g; Protein: 6g;
Cholesterol: 4mg; Sodium: 298mg

108.Red Potatoes with Chives and Garlic

Yield: 3 Servings

Total Time: 25 Minutes

Prep Time: 10 Minutes

Cook Time: 15 Minutes

Ingredients

- 1 pound red potatoes, unpeeled
- 1 bay leaf
- 2 tablespoons butter, melted
- ½ cup water
- 1 garlic clove, peeled
- 1 tablespoon cream cheese
- 2 tablespoons chives, minced
- Salt and black pepper, to taste

Directions:

1. Put the butter, bay leaf and garlic in the Instant Pot and select "Sauté".
2. Sauté for 2 minutes and add red potatoes, water, chives, salt and black pepper.
3. Set the Instant Pot to "Manual" at high pressure for 10 minutes.
4. Release the pressure naturally and top with cream cheese.

Nutritional Information per Serving:

Calories: 188; Total Fat: 9.1g; Carbs: 24.7g; Sugars: 1.6g; Protein: 3.3g; Cholesterol: 24mg; Sodium: 75mg

109.Cheesy Polenta Squares

Yield: 12 Servings

Total Time: 30 Minutes

Prep Time: 10 Minutes

Cook Time: 20 Minutes

Ingredients

- 4 cups yellow cornmeal
- 8 cups water
- 1 cup Parmesan cheese
- 1 cup butter
- 2 teaspoons salt
- 1 teaspoon black pepper

Directions:

1. Put the water, yellow cornmeal, 4 tablespoons butter and salt in the Instant Pot.
2. Set the Instant Pot to "Manual" at high pressure for 10 minutes.
3. Release the pressure naturally and stir in Parmesan cheese, black pepper and ½ cup unsalted butter.
4. Put this mixture in the baking dish.
5. Place the trivet in the Instant Pot and transfer the baking dish on it.
6. Set the instant pot to "Manual" and cook for 17 minutes at high pressure.
7. Release the pressure naturally and

Nutritional Information per Serving:

Calories: 291; Total Fat: 17.3g; Carbs: 31.5g; Sugars: 0.3g; Protein: 4.2g; Cholesterol: 42mg; Sodium: 537mg

110.Cheesy Burrito Bites

Yield: 4 Servings

Total Time: 25 Minutes

Prep Time: 15 Minutes

Cook Time: 10 Minutes

Ingredients

- 4 oz. tofu, browned and chopped
- ¼ cup purple onion
- ¼ cup cilantro, chopped
- ½ teaspoon salt
- ½ cup cooked black beans
- ¼ cup cheddar cheese, shredded
- 1 tablespoon olive oil
- 4 oz. Mexican rice, cooked
- ¼ cup tomatoes, diced
- ¼ cup water
- 2 giant flour tortillas
- ½ avocado, peeled and sliced

Directions:

1. Put the olive oil and tofu in the Instant Pot and select "Sauté".
2. Sauté for 2 minutes and add Mexican rice.
3. Dish out and keep aside.
4. Put the onions, cilantro, tomatoes and salt in the Instant Pot.
5. Set the Instant Pot to "Manual" at high pressure for 6 minutes.
6. Release the pressure naturally and mix with the rice mixture.

7. Put the spoonful of rice mixture, some avocado slices, 1 tablespoon of black beans and shredded cheddar cheese in a tortilla sheet and roll it tightly.

8. Repeat this process with the other tortilla sheet.

Nutritional Information per Serving:

Calories: 381; Total Fat: 14g; Carbs: 52.7g; Sugars: 1.5g; Protein: 14g; Cholesterol: 7mg; Sodium: 409mg

Scrumptious Dessert Recipes

111.Carrot Pudding

Yield: 6 Servings

Total Time: 25 Minutes

Prep Time: 10 Minutes

Cook Time: 15 Minutes

Ingredients

- 1 pound carrots, peeled and grated
- ½ cup full fat milk
- 2 tablespoons unsalted butter
- 20 almonds, peeled
- 3 green cardamoms, powdered
- 1 cup condensed milk
- 2 tablespoons cream cheese

Directions:

1. Put the butter and cardamoms in the Instant Pot and select "Sauté".
2. Sauté for 30 seconds and add carrots, full fat milk and condensed milk.
3. Set the Instant Pot to "Manual" at high pressure for 12 minutes.
4. Release the pressure naturally and add cream cheese.
5. Garnish with almonds and serve in pudding glasses or bowls.

Nutritional Information per Serving:

Calories: 277; Total Fat: 11.9g; Carbs: 38.6g; Sugars: 31.6g; Protein: 6.3g;

Cholesterol: 31mg; Sodium: 154mg

112.Sweet Potato Dessert Risotto

Yield: 6 Servings

Total Time: 28 Minutes

Prep Time: 10 Minutes

Cook Time: 18 Minutes

Ingredients

- ½ cup risotto rice
- ½ cup coconut milk
- 1 tablespoon butter
- ¾ cup water
- ½ teaspoon vanilla extract
- ½ teaspoon cardamom powder
- ½ cup raisins
- ½ cup evaporated milk
- ¼ cup honey
- ½ teaspoon cinnamon powder
- ½ teaspoon salt
- 1 sweet potato, grated
- ½ cup almonds, roasted and grated

Directions:

1. Put the butter and melt it in the Instant Pot.
2. Add evaporated milk, coconut milk, honey and water.
3. Mix well and add cardamom powder, cinnamon powder, vanilla extract and salt.

4. Stir well and add risotto rice and grated sweet potato.

5. Set the Instant Pot to "Manual" at high pressure for 12 minutes.

6. Release the pressure naturally and add raisins.

7. Let it simmer for 4 minutes and top with roasted almonds.

Nutritional Information per Serving:
Calories: 291; Total Fat: 12.4g; Carbs: 42.5g; Sugars: 23.2g; Protein: 5.5g;

Cholesterol: 11mg; Sodium: 243mg

113.Crème Coffee Brûlée

Yield: 3 Servings

Total Time: 30 Minutes

Prep Time: 10 Minutes

Cook Time: 20 Minutes

Ingredients

- 4 egg yolks

- 1 cup heavy cream

- ½ teaspoon coffee powder

- Pinch of salt

- ¼ cup granulated sugar

- ½ teaspoon vanilla extract

- 3 tablespoons superfine sugar

- 1 cup water

Directions:

1. Whisk egg yolks, granulated sugar and salt in a bowl.

2. Add coffee powder, heavy cream and vanilla extract and whisk gently.

3. Put this mixture in 3 custard cups and cover tightly with an aluminium foil.

4. Arrange the trivet in the Instant Pot and add water.

5. Place the custard cups on the trivet and lock the lid.

6. Set the instant pot to "Manual" and cook for 6 minutes at high pressure.

7. Release the pressure naturally for 10 minutes and remove the cups.

8. Refrigerate the crème Brûlée and sprinkle superfine sugar.

9. Burn this sprinkled sugar for 2 minutes using a blow torch.

Nutritional Information per Serving:
Calories: 337; Total Fat: 20.8g; Carbs: 35.4g; Sugars: 33.6g; Protein: 4.4g;

Cholesterol: 335mg; Sodium: 79mg

114.Red Wine Poached Pears

Yield: 3 Servings

Total Time: 40 Minutes

Prep Time: 10 Minutes

Cook Time: 30 Minutes

Ingredients

- 3 firm pears, peeled and stem attached
- ½ bottle red wine
- 2 cloves
- ½ teaspoon ginger,grated
- ½ cinnamon, grated
- 1 bay laurel leaf

- 1 cup granulated sugar

Directions:

1. Put all the ingredients in the Instant Pot and lock the lid.

2. Set the instant pot to "Manual" and cook for 8 minutes at high pressure.

3. Release the pressure naturally for 10 minutes and dish out the pears.

4. Let the mixture simmer for 10 more minutes to reduce its consistency.

5. Drizzle the red wine sauce on pears and serve.

Nutritional Information per Serving:
Calories: 434; Total Fat: 0.38g; Carbs: 101.7g; Sugars: 87.9g; Protein: 1.2g;

Cholesterol: 0mg; Sodium: 6mg

115.Cherry Apple Risotto

Yield: 4 Servings

Total Time: 20 Minutes

Prep Time: 10 Minutes

Cook Time: 10 Minutes

Ingredients

- 1 tablespoon butter

- ¾ cup Arborio rice, soaked

- 1 apple, diced

- 2 pinches salt

- ¾teaspoon cinnamon powder

- ¼ cup brown sugar

- ½ cup apple juice

- 1½ cups milk
- ¼ cup dried cherries
- 1½ tablespoons almonds, roasted and sliced
- ¼ cup whipped cream

Directions:

1. Put the butter and rice in the Instant Pot and select "Sauté".
2. Sauté for 3 minutes and add rest of the ingredients.
3. Set the Instant Pot to "Manual" at high pressure for 7 minutes.
4. Release the pressure quickly and add dried cherries, almonds and whipped cream.

Nutritional Information per Serving:
Calories: 317; Total Fat: 8.5g; Carbs: 54.9g; Sugars: 21.8g; Protein: 6.2g;

Cholesterol: 23mg; Sodium: 151mg

116.Coconut Chocolate Fondue

Yield: 4 Servings

Total Time: 15 Minutes

Prep Time: 10 Minutes

Cook Time: 5 Minutes

Ingredients

- 200 g Swiss bittersweet chocolate (70%)
- 200 g coconut cream
- 2teaspoons coconut milk powder
- 2 teaspoons sugar

- 2 teaspoons coconut essence
- 2 cups water

Directions:

1. Mix chocolate, sugar and coconut cream in a ceramic pot.
2. Arrange the trivet in the Instant Pot and add water.
3. Place the ceramic pot on the trivet and lock the lid.
4. Set the instant pot to "Manual" and cook for 3 minutes at high pressure.
5. Release the pressure naturally and add coconut essence and coconut milk powder.
6. Stir gently and serve in fondue pot.

Nutritional Information per Serving:
Calories: 266; Total Fat: 21.4g; Carbs: 16.8g; Sugars: 14.2g; Protein: 2.7g; Cholesterol: 0mg; Sodium: 26mg

117. Strawberry Rhubarb Tarts

Yield: 12 Servings

Total Time: 17 Minutes

Prep Time: 10 Minutes

Cook Time: 7 Minutes

Ingredients

- 1 cup water
- 1 pound rhubarb, cut into ½ inch pieces
- ½ pound strawberries
- ¼ cup crystallized ginger, chopped

- Readymade 12 tart shells, short crust
- ½ cup honey
- ½ cup whipped cream

Directions:

1. Put all the ingredients in the Instant Pot except the tart shells and whipped cream.
2. Set the instant pot to "Manual" and cook for 5 minutes at high pressure.
3. Release the pressure naturally and fill the mixture in the tart shells.
4. Top with whipped cream and serve.

Nutritional Information per Serving:
Calories: 163; Total Fat: 6.2g; Carbs: 26.2g; Sugars: 14g; Protein: 1.6g;
Cholesterol: 11mg; Sodium: 90mg

118.Dulce De Leche

Yield: 2 Servings

Total Time: 55 Minutes

Prep Time: 10 Minutes

Cook Time: 45 Minutes

Ingredients

- 2 cans(14 oz.) sweetened condensed milk
- 16 cups water
- 2 (16 oz.) canning jar with lid

Directions:

1. Pour condensed milk in the canning jar, place the lid and screw on the ring.

2. Arrange the trivet in the Instant Pot and add water.

3. Place the canning jar on the trivet and lock the lid.

4. Set the instant pot to "Manual" and cook for 30 minutes at high pressure.

5. Release the pressure naturally for 15 minutes and let it cool.

Nutritional Information per Serving:
Calories: 61; Total Fat: 1.7g; Carbs: 10.4g; Sugars: 10.4g; Protein: 1.5g;

Cholesterol: 6mg; Sodium: 81mg

119.Hazelnut Flan

Yield: 10 Servings

Total Time: 20 Minutes

Prep Time: 10 Minutes

Cook Time: 10 Minutes

Ingredients

- 6 eggs

- ½ cups granulated sugar

- 4 cups whole milk

- 2 teaspoons vanilla extract

- 4 egg yolks

- ¼ teaspoon salt

- 1 cup whipping cream

- 8 tablespoons hazelnut syrup

- ½ cup caramel

- 2 cups water

Directions:

1. Whisk together eggs, egg yolks, salt and sugar in a bowl.
2. Boil milk and add gradually to the egg mixture.
3. Add vanilla extract, whipping cream and hazelnut syrup to this mixture.
4. Put the caramel in the custard cups and add the hazelnut mixture in them.
5. Arrange the trivet in the Instant Pot and add water.
6. Place the custard cups on the trivet and lock the lid.
7. Set the instant pot to "Manual" and cook for 8 minutes at high pressure.
8. Release the pressure naturally and serve after refrigerating it for 3 hours.

Nutritional Information per Serving:

Calories: 244; Total Fat: 14.2g; Carbs: 21.4g; Sugars: 20.32g; Protein: 8.5g; Cholesterol: 206mg; Sodium: 160mg

120.Peanut Butter Custard

Yield: 10 Servings

Total Time: 20 Minutes

Prep Time: 10 Minutes

Cook Time: 10 Minutes

Ingredients

- 1 cup caramel
- 4 whole eggs
- 4 egg yolks
- ½ cup granulated sugar

- ¼ teaspoon salt
- 4 cups whole milk
- 1 cup whipping cream
- 2 teaspoons vanilla extract
- 8tablespoons peanut butter
- 2 cups water

Directions:

1. Whisk together eggs, egg yolks, salt and sugar in a bowl.
2. Boil milk and add gradually to the egg mixture.
3. Add vanilla extract, whipping cream and peanut butter to this mixture.
4. Put the caramel in the custard cups and add the peanut butter mixture in them.
5. Arrange the trivet in the Instant Pot and add water.
6. Place the custard cups on the trivet and lock the lid.
7. Set the instant pot to "Manual" and cook for 10 minutes at high pressure.
8. Release the pressure naturally and serve after refrigerating it for 3 hours.

Nutritional Information per Serving:

Calories: 276; Total Fat: 17.3g; Carbs: 21.9g; Sugars: 20.1g; Protein: 10.1g;

Cholesterol: 173mg; Sodium: 203mg

121.Beetroot Pudding

Yield: 6 Servings

Total Time: 25 Minutes

Prep Time: 10 Minutes

Cook Time: 15 Minutes

Ingredients

- 1 pound green beetroot, freshly grated
- ½ cup full fat milk
- 2 tablespoons unsalted butter
- 18 almonds, peeled
- 1 teaspoon cardamom powder
- ½ cup condensed milk
- 3 tablespoons mascarpone cheese
- 3 tablespoons whipped cream

Directions:

1. Put the butter and cardamom powder in the Instant Pot and select "Sauté".
2. Sauté for 30 seconds and add beetroot,full fat milk and condensed milk.
3. Set the Instant Pot to "Manual" at high pressure for 12 minutes.
4. Release the pressure naturally and add mascarpone cheese.
5. Garnish with almonds and top with whipped cream.

Nutritional Information per Serving:

Calories: 195; Total Fat: 11.2g; Carbs: 19.3g; Sugars: 15.1g; Protein: 5.4g;

Cholesterol: 32mg; Sodium: 79mg

122.Cranberry Apple Rice Pudding

Yield: 4 Servings

Total Time: 20 Minutes

Prep Time: 10 Minutes

Cook Time: 10 Minutes

Ingredients

- ¾ cup Arborio rice, soaked
- 2 pinches salt
- ¼ cup brown sugar
- 1½ cups milk
- 1½ tablespoons almonds, roasted and sliced
- 1 tablespoon butter
- 1 apple, diced
- ¾ teaspoon cinnamon powder
- ½ cup apple juice
- ¼ cup dried cranberries
- ¼ cup whipped cream

Directions:

1. Put the butter and rice in the Instant Pot and select "Sauté".
2. Sauté for 4 minutes and add rest of the ingredients.
3. Set the Instant Pot to "Manual" at high pressure for 8 minutes.
4. Release the pressure quickly and add dried cranberries, almonds and whipped cream.

Nutritional Information per Serving:

Calories: 317; Total Fat: 8.5g; Carbs: 5.9g; Sugars: 21.8g; Protein: 6.2g; Cholesterol: 23mg; Sodium: 151mg

123.Chocolate Pudding

Yield: 6 Servings

Total Time: 33 Minutes

Prep Time: 10 Minutes

Cook Time: 23 Minutes

Ingredients

- 2 tablespoons dark chocolate, grated
- 100 g golden castor sugar
- 1 teaspoon vanilla extract
- 1 tablespoon cocoa powder
- 100 g butter
- 2 eggs
- 100 g self-rising flour
- 2 cups water

Directions:

1. Mix together butter, sugar, eggs and vanilla extract in a bowl.
2. Sift self-rising flour, dark chocolate and cocoa powder in the eggs mixture.
3. Arrange the trivet in the Instant Pot and add water.
4. Put the bowl on the trivet and lock the lid.
5. Set the Instant Pot to "Manual" at low pressure for 20 minutes.
6. Release the pressure naturally and refrigerate before serving.

Nutritional Information per Serving:
Calories: 287; Total Fat: 16.3g; Carbs: 31.9g; Sugars: 18.3g; Protein: 4.2g;

Cholesterol: 91mg; Sodium: 30mg

124.Dark Chocolate Fondue

Yield: 3 Servings

Total Time: 15 Minutes

Prep Time: 10 Minutes

Cook Time: 5 Minutes

Ingredients

- 150 g Swiss bittersweet chocolate (70%)

- 150 g fresh cream

- 1½ teaspoons Amaretto Liquor

- 1½ teaspoons sugar

- 1½ cups water

Directions:

1. Mix chocolate, sugar and fresh cream in a ceramic pot.

2. Arrange the trivet in the Instant Pot and add water.

3. Place the ceramic pot on the trivet and lock the lid.

4. Set the instant pot to "Manual" and cook for 3 minutes at high pressure.

5. Release the pressure naturally and add Amaretto Liquor.

6. Stir gently and serve in fondue pot.

Nutritional Information per Serving:

Calories: 399; Total Fat: 27.4g; Carbs: 38.3g; Sugars: 31g; Protein: 4.1g; Cholesterol: 38mg; Sodium: 86mg

125.White Chocolate Orange Fondue

Yield: 6 Servings

Total Time: 15 Minutes

Prep Time: 10 Minutes

Cook Time: 5 Minutes

Ingredients

- 250 g Swiss white chocolate
- 250 g fresh cream
- 2½ teaspoons candied orange peel, chopped finely
- 2½ teaspoons sugar
- 2½ teaspoons orange essence
- 2½ cups water

Directions:

1. Mix white chocolate, sugar and fresh cream in a ceramic pot.
2. Arrange the trivet in the Instant Pot and add water.
3. Place the ceramic pot on the trivet and lock the lid.
4. Set the instant pot to "Manual" and cook for 4 minutes at high pressure.
5. Release the pressure naturally and add candied orange peel and orange essence.
6. Stir gently and serve in fondue pot.

Nutritional Information per Serving:

Calories: 379; Total Fat: 22.6g; Carbs: 38g; Sugars: 34.9g; Protein: 3.8g; Cholesterol: 40mg; Sodium: 105mg

126.Instant Pot Baked Apple

Yield: 3 Servings

Total Time: 15 Minutes

Prep Time: 3 Minutes

Cook Time: 12 Minutes

Ingredients

- 3 apples, cored
- ¼ cup raisins
- ½ cup red wine
- ¼ cup sugar
- ½ teaspoon cinnamon powder

Directions:

1. Put all the ingredients in the Instant Pot and lock the lid.
2. Set the instant pot to "Manual" and cook for 10 minutes at high pressure.
3. Release the pressure naturally and serve hot.

Nutritional Information per Serving:

Calories: 247; Total Fat: 0.5g; Carbs: 58.1g; Sugars: 47.3g; Protein: 1g;

Cholesterol: 0mg; Sodium: 5mg

127.Apple and Ricotta Cake

Yield: 6 Servings

Total Time: 15 Minutes

Prep Time: 10 Minutes

Cook Time: 5 Minutes

Ingredients

- 1 cup all-purpose flour
- 1 cup ricotta cheese
- 2 apples, 1 sliced and 1 diced
- 1 tablespoon lemon juice
- 1 egg
- 4 tablespoons olive oil
- 1 teaspoon vanilla extract
- 2 teaspoons baking powder
- ½ cup sugar
- ¼ teaspoon cinnamon powder
- 1 teaspoon baking soda
- 2 cups water

Directions:

1. Mix together egg, sugar, ricotta cheese, vanilla extract and olive oil.
2. Add cinnamon powder, flour, baking powder and baking soda using the sifter and mix thoroughly.
3. Cover the apples with lemon juice and place in the cake tin.
4. Pour the above mixture in the cake tin above the apples.
5. Arrange the trivet in the Instant Pot and add water.

6. Place the ceramic pot on the trivet and lock the lid.

7. Set the instant pot to "Manual" and cook for 20 minutes at high pressure.

8. Release the pressure naturally and serve hot.

Nutritional Information per Serving:
Calories: 329; Total Fat: 13.7g; Carbs: 45.9g; Sugars: 24.8g; Protein: 8g; Cholesterol: 40mg; Sodium: 276mg

128.Chocolate Hazelnut Lava Cake

Yield: 4 Servings

Total Time: 20 Minutes

Prep Time: 10 Minutes

Cook Time: 10 Minutes

Ingredients

- ½ cup all-purpose flour
- ¼ cup hazelnut paste
- 2 tablespoons fresh cream
- ½ cup sugar
- 1 pinch salt
- 4tablespoons bitter cocoa powder
- ½ teaspoon baking powder
- 1 medium egg
- ¾ cup milk
- ¼ cup olive oil
- 1 cup water

Directions:

1. Mix together flour, sugar, salt, baking powder and cocoa powder in a bowl.

2. Add egg, olive oil, milk and whisk well.

3. Put this mixture into 4 small ramekins and put hazelnut paste in the centre.

4. Arrange the trivet in the Instant Pot and add water.

5. Place the ramekins on the trivet and lock the lid.

6. Set the instant pot to "Manual" and cook for 10 minutes at high pressure.

7. Release the pressure naturally and serve hot.

Nutritional Information per Serving:

Calories: 355; Total Fat: 19.3g; Carbs: 44.4g; Sugars: 28.2g; Protein: 6.4g; Cholesterol: 46mg; Sodium: 80mg

129.Pear and Apple Clafoutis

Yield: 8 Servings

Total Time: 35 Minutes

Prep Time: 10 Minutes

Cook Time: 25 Minutes

Ingredients

- 2 eggs
- 1 cup apples, chopped
- 1 cup pears, chopped
- ¾ cup sugar
- 2 cups all-purpose flour
- 1 cup milk

- 1 tablespoon vanilla extract
- 2 tablespoons powdered sugar
- 2 cups water
- Oil, for greasing

Directions

1. Oil the wax paper and place it well in the tin.
2. Mix together eggs, vanilla extract and sugar in a bowl.
3. Add milk and flour gradually and pour in the tin.
4. Top with chopped fruits and cover tightly with the foil.
5. Arrange the trivet in the Instant Pot and add water.
6. Place the tin on the trivet and lock the lid.
7. Set the instant pot to "Manual" and cook for 20 minutes at high pressure.
8. Release the pressure naturally and serve hot.

Nutritional Information per Serving:

Calories: 254; Total Fat: 2.1g; Carbs: 53.3g; Sugars: 27.3g; Protein: 5.8g; Cholesterol: 43mg; Sodium: 33mg

130.Almond and Cardamom Tapioca Pudding

Yield: 4 Servings

Total Time: 15 Minutes

Prep Time: 10 Minutes

Cook Time: 5 Minutes

Ingredients

- 50 g tapioca pearls
- ½ cup water
- ½ teaspoon cardamom powder
- 1 cup whole milk
- ½ cup sugar
- ½ cup almonds, roasted

Directions:

1. Mix together tapioca pearls, milk, sugar, cardamom powder and water in a bowl.
2. Arrange the trivet in the Instant Pot and add 2 cups water.
3. Place the bowl on the trivet and lock the lid.
4. Set the instant pot to "Manual" and cook for 8 minutes at high pressure.
5. Release the pressure naturally and garnish with almonds.

Nutritional Information per Serving:

Calories: 245; Total Fat: 7.9g; Carbs: 41.6g; Sugars: 29.1g; Protein: 4.5g; Cholesterol: 6mg; Sodium: 26mg

Hot and Cold Beverages Recipes

131.Agua De Jamaica Hibiscus Tea

Yield: 8 Servings

Total Time: 20 Minutes

Prep Time: 5 Minutes

Cook Time: 15 Minutes

Ingredients

- 1 cup hibiscus flowers, dried

- 2 quarts water

- 1 cup sugar

- ½teaspoon ginger, minced

- 1 cinnamon stick

- 2 teaspoons lime juice

Directions:

1. Put all the ingredients in the Instant Pot except lime juice.

2. Set the instant pot to "Manual" and cook for 5 minutes at high pressure.

3. Release the pressure naturally for 10 minutes and decant the liquid into a glass pitcher.

4. Add lime juice to the pitcher and serve after chilling.

Nutritional Information per Serving:

Calories: 95; Total Fat: 0g; Carbs: 25.4g; Sugars: 25g; Protein: 4g; Cholesterol: 0mg; Sodium: 7mg

132.Blackberry Drink

Yield: 4 Servings

Total Time: 20 Minutes

Prep Time: 5 Minutes

Cook Time: 15 Minutes

Ingredients

- 2 cups blackberries
- 1 bottle water
- 1 cup white sugar
- 1 lemon, roundly sliced

Directions:

1. Put all the ingredients in the Instant Pot except lemon.
2. Set the instant pot to "Manual" and cook for 10 minutes at high pressure.
3. Release the pressure naturally and decant the liquid into serving glasses.
4. Add lemon slices to the serving glasses and serve after chilling.

Nutritional Information per Serving:

Calories: 223; Total Fat: 0.4g; Carbs: 58.3g; Sugars: 53.9g; Protein: 1.2g; Cholesterol: 0mg; Sodium: 3mg

133.Spiked Cider

Yield: 3 Servings

Total Time: 20 Minutes

Prep Time: 5 Minutes

Cook Time: 15 Minutes

Ingredients

- 3 apples, sliced
- 1 orange, sliced
- ¼ teaspoon nutmeg
- ½ cup fresh cranberries
- 2 cinnamon sticks
- 3 cups water
- 3 tablespoons organic cassava syrup

Directions:

1. Put all the ingredients in the Instant Pot.
2. Set the instant pot to "Manual" and cook for 10 minutes at high pressure.
3. Release the pressure naturally and strain the mixture using mesh strainer.

Nutritional Information per Serving:

Calories: 162; Total Fat: 0.6g; Carbs: 41.7g; Sugars: 29.7g; Protein: 1.3g; Cholesterol: 0mg; Sodium: 9mg

134.Berry Kombucha

Yield: 6 Servings

Total Time: 12 Minutes

Prep Time: 2 Minutes

Cook Time: 10 Minutes

Ingredients

- 4 cups sparkling water
- 1 cup frozen mixed berries
- 4 cups kombucha

Directions:

1. Put all the ingredients in the Instant Pot.
2. Set the instant pot to "Manual" and cook for 8 minutes at high pressure.
3. Release the pressure naturally and serve hot.

Nutritional Information per Serving:

Calories: 31; Total Fat: 0.1g; Carbs: 7g; Sugars: 2.9g; Protein: 0.2g; Cholesterol: 0mg; Sodium: 7mg

135.Berry Lemonade Tea

Yield: 4 Servings

Total Time: 20 Minutes

Prep Time: 5 Minutes

Cook Time: 15 Minutes

Ingredients

- 3 tea bags

- 2 cups natural lemonade
- 1 cup frozen mixed berries
- 2 cups water
- 1 lemon, sliced

Directions:

1. Put all the ingredients in the Instant Pot.
2. Set the instant pot to "Manual" and cook for 12 minutes at high pressure.
3. Release the pressure naturally and strain the mixture.

Nutritional Information per Serving:
Calories: 8; Total Fat: 0.2g; Carbs: 21.6g; Sugars: 18.4g; Protein: 0.4g;

Cholesterol: 0mg; Sodium: 4mg

136.Ginger Lemon Tea

Yield: 4 Servings

Total Time: 27 Minutes

Prep Time: 10 Minutes

Cook Time: 17 Minutes

Ingredients

- 3 cups water
- 1 (1-inch) piece fresh ginger, peeled
- 1 cup fresh lemon juice
- 1 teaspoon ginger powder
- 1 tablespoon fenugreek seeds

Directions:

1. Put all the ingredients in the Instant Pot.
2. Set the instant pot to "Manual" and cook for 15 minutes at high pressure.
3. Release the pressure naturally and strain the mixture.

Nutritional Information per Serving:

Calories: 27; Total Fat: 0.7g; Carbs: 3.5g; Sugars: 1.3g; Protein: 1.2g; Cholesterol: 0mg; Sodium: 20mg

137.Spiced Ginger Cider

Yield: 12 Servings

Total Time: 25 Minutes

Prep Time: 10 Minutes

Cook Time: 15 Minutes

Ingredients

- 2 small apples, peeled
- 12 cups apple cider
- 2 whole allspice
- 2 teaspoons fresh ginger
- 4 teaspoons orange zest
- 2 teaspoons cinnamon powder
- 4 whole cloves
- ½ teaspoon ground nutmeg

Directions:

1. Put all the ingredients in the Instant Pot.
2. Set the instant pot to "Manual" and cook for 13 minutes at high pressure.

3. Release the pressure naturally and strain the mixture.

Nutritional Information per Serving:

Calories: 141; Total Fat: 0.6g; Carbs: 35.2g; Sugars: 31g; Protein: 0.4g; Cholesterol: 0mg; Sodium: 10mg

138.Swedish Glögg

Yield: 1 Serving

Total Time: 23 Minutes

Prep Time: 5 Minutes

Cook Time: 18 Minutes

Ingredients

- ½ cup orange juice
- ½ cup water
- 1 (½-inch) piece fresh ginger
- 1 whole clove
- 1 cardamom pods, opened
- 2 tablespoons orange zest
- 1 cinnamon stick
- 1 whole allspice
- 1 vanilla bean

Directions:

1. Put all the ingredients in the Instant Pot.
2. Set the instant pot to "Manual" and cook for 15 minutes at high pressure.
3. Release the pressure naturally and strain the mixture.

Nutritional Information per Serving:

Calories: 194; Total Fat: 3.1g; Carbs: 41.4g; Sugars: 10.5g; Protein: 1.7g; Cholesterol: 10mg; Sodium: 64mg

139.Spiced Orange Apple Cider

Yield: 3 Servings

Total Time: 17 Minutes

Prep Time: 5 Minutes

Cook Time: 12 Minutes

Ingredients

- 3 cups apple juice
- 1½ tablespoons lemon juice
- 1 cup orange juice
- 2 tablespoons whole allspice
- ½ teaspoon cinnamon powder
- ½ apple, sliced
- ½ orange, sliced

Directions:

1. Put all the ingredients in the Instant Pot except apple and orange slices.
2. Set the instant pot to "Manual" and cook for 10 minutes at high pressure.
3. Release the pressure naturally and serve with apple and orange slices.

Nutritional Information per Serving:

Calories: 196; Total Fat: 1g; Carbs: 48.4g; Sugars: 37.8g; Protein: 1.5g; Cholesterol: 0mg; Sodium: 16mg

140.Hot Mulled Cider

Yield: 4 Servings

Total Time: 17 Minutes

Prep Time: 5 Minutes

Cook Time: 12 Minutes

Ingredients

- 3 cups apple cider
- 1½ tablespoons cinnamon powder
- 1 (½-inch) piece ginger
- ½ cup apricot nectar
- ½ cup orange juice
- ½ teaspoon pumpkin pie spice
- 3 whole cloves
- ½ orange, sliced

Directions:

1. Put all the ingredients in the Instant Pot except orange slices.

2. Set the instant pot to "Manual" and cook for 12 minutes at high pressure.

3. Release the pressure naturally and serve with orange slices.

Nutritional Information per Serving:

Calories: 136; Total Fat: 0.7g; Carbs: 33.4g; Sugars: 25.1g; Protein: 0.8g;

Cholesterol: 0mg; Sodium: 11mg

141.Spiced Pear Cider

Yield: 2 Servings

Total Time: 15 Minutes

Prep Time: 10 Minutes

Cook Time: 5 Minutes

Ingredients

- 4 whole allspice
- 2 whole cloves
- 1 (3-inch) cinnamon stick
- ½ cup pear nectar
- 2 cups unsweetened pear juice

Directions:

1. Put all the ingredients in the Instant Pot.
2. Set the instant pot to "Manual" and cook for 15 minutes at high pressure.
3. Release the pressure naturally and serve hot.

Nutritional Information per Serving:

Calories: 124; Total Fat: 0.8g; Carbs: 30.9g; Sugars: 21.5g; Protein: 0.4g;

Cholesterol: 0mg; Sodium: 11mg

142.Fruit Punch

Yield: 5 Servings

Total Time: 13 Minutes

Prep Time: 3 Minutes

Cook Time: 10 Minutes

Ingredients

- 1 cup apple juice
- 1 cup cranberry juice
- ½ cup apricot juice
- ½ cup lemon juice
- ½-inch cinnamon stick
- 1 cup hot brewed tea
- 1 cup orange juice
- 6 whole cloves

Directions:

1. Put all the ingredients in the Instant Pot.
2. Set the instant pot to "Manual" and cook for 8 minutes at high pressure.
3. Release the pressure naturally and serve after chilling.

Nutritional Information per Serving:

Calories: 80; Total Fat: 0.9g; Carbs: 17.1g; Sugars: 12.3g; Protein: 0.7g;

Cholesterol: 0mg; Sodium: 14mg

143.Homemade Lemonade

Yield: 3 Servings

Total Time: 20 Minutes

Prep Time: 6 Minutes

Cook Time: 14 Minutes

Ingredients

- 1½ cups fresh lemon juice

- 1-inch cinnamon stick
- 1½ cup water
- 3 mint leaves

Directions:

1. Put all the ingredients in the Instant Pot.

2. Set the instant pot to "Manual" and cook for 12 minutes at high pressure.

3. Release the pressure naturally and serve after chilling.

Nutritional Information per Serving:

Calories: 114; Total Fat: 3.7g; Carbs: 11g; Sugars: 9.4g; Protein: 4g; Cholesterol: 0mg; Sodium: 106mg

144.Red Cherry Cider

Yield: 12 Servings

Total Time: 30 Minutes

Prep Time: 10 Minutes

Cook Time: 20 Minutes

Ingredients

- 8 cups cherry juice
- 4 cups apple juice
- 4 (1-inch) cinnamon sticks

Directions:

1. Put all the ingredients in the Instant Pot.

2. Set the instant pot to "Manual" and cook for 20 minutes at high pressure.

3. Release the pressure naturally and serve hot.

Nutritional Information per Serving:
Calories: 96; Total Fat: 0.1g; Carbs: 23.8g; Sugars: 8g; Protein: 0.3g;

Cholesterol: 0mg; Sodium: 12mg

145Red Hot Punch

Yield: 8 Servings

Total Time: 25 Minutes

Prep Time: 5 Minutes

Cook Time: 20 Minutes

Ingredients

- 2 cups apple juice
- 2 cups hot brewed tea
- 2 cups pineapple juice
- 8 tablespoons Frank's Red Hot
- 2 cups orange juice
- 8 mint leaves

Directions:

1. Put all the ingredients in the Instant Pot.
2. Set the instant pot to "Manual" and cook for 18 minutes at high pressure.
3. Release the pressure naturally and serve hot.

Nutritional Information per Serving:
Calories: 100; Total Fat: 0.4g; Carbs: 23.6g; Sugars: 17.4g; Protein: 1.1g;

Cholesterol: 0mg; Sodium: 428mg

146.Spiced Peachy Cider

Yield: 4 Servings

Total Time: 20 Minutes

Prep Time: 5 Minutes

Cook Time: 15 Minutes

Ingredients

- 3 cups peach nectar
- 1 teaspoon ground ginger
- ½ teaspoon ground nutmeg
- 1½ cups apple juice
- ½ teaspoon ground cinnamon
- 4 fresh orange slices

Directions:

1. Put all the ingredients in the Instant Pot except orange slices.
2. Set the instant pot to "Manual" and cook for 14 minutes at high pressure.
3. Release the pressure naturally and add orange slices.

Nutritional Information per Serving:

Calories: 205; Total Fat: 0.8g; Carbs: 50.2g; Sugars: 44g; Protein: 1.4g; Cholesterol: 0mg; Sodium: 14mg

147.Pomegranate Punch

Yield: 3 Servings

Total Time: 25 Minutes

Prep Time: 10 Minutes

Cook Time: 15 Minutes

Ingredients

- 1 cup pomegranate juice
- ¾ cup brewed tea
- 3 whole cloves
- 1 cup unsweetened apple juice
- ¾ cup lemon juice
- 1-inch cinnamon stick

Directions:

1. Put all the ingredients in the Instant Pot.
2. Set the instant pot to "Manual" and cook for 12 minutes at high pressure.
3. Release the pressure naturally and serve chilled.

Nutritional Information per Serving:
Calories: 113; Total Fat: 1g; Carbs: 25.4g; Sugars: 21g; Protein: 0.7g;

Cholesterol: 0mg; Sodium: 25mg

148.Instant Horchata

Yield: 2 Servings

Total Time: 17 Minutes

Prep Time: 2 Minutes

Cook Time: 15 Minutes

Ingredients

2 cups unsweetened rice milk

1 cinnamon stick

8 tablespoons sugar

Directions:

1. Put all the ingredients in the Instant Pot.

2. Set the instant pot to "Manual" and cook for 5 minutes at high pressure.

3. Release the pressure naturally for 10 minutes and serve hot.

Nutritional Information per Serving:

Calories: 228; Total Fat: 2g; Carbs: 58.9g; Sugars: 48g; Protein: 1.1g;

Cholesterol: 0mg; Sodium: 135mg

149.Mango Yogurt Lassi

Yield: 3 Servings

Total Time: 25 Minutes

Prep Time: 5 Minutes

Cook Time: 20 Minutes

Ingredients

- 2 cups mango

- 1 cup yogurt

- 3 tablespoons honey

- 1 cup water

Directions:

1. Put all the ingredients in the Instant Pot.

2. Set the instant pot to "Manual" and cook for 10 minutes at high pressure.

3. Release the pressure naturally for 10 minutes and serve chilled.

Nutritional Information per Serving:

Calories: 188; Total Fat: 1.4g; Carbs: 39.5g; Sugars: 38g; Protein: 5.6g; Cholesterol: 5mg; Sodium: 61mg

150. Rose Milk

Yield: 3 Servings

Total Time: 15 Minutes

Prep Time: 5 Minutes

Cook Time: 10 Minutes

Ingredients

- 3 cups full fat milk
- 2 tablespoons sugar
- ½ cup raw cashews
- ½ cup dried rose petals
- 6 drops red food coloring

Directions:

1. Put all the ingredients in the Instant Pot.
2. Set the instant pot to "Manual" and cook for 10 minutes at high pressure.
3. Release the pressure naturally for 10 minutes and strain the mixture.

Nutritional Information per Serving:

Calories: 241; Total Fat: 10.6g; Carbs: 27.5g; Sugars: 21.1g; Protein: 12.5g; Cholesterol: 5mg; Sodium: 129mg

Conclusion

If you want to have delicious and healthy vegetarian diet using an instant pot, than this is the solution for your problem. This recipe book not only provides you with 150 vegetarian recipes from almost are food groups, but also the procedure to cook them in an instant pot. Cooking had never been this easy for you than before, so don't waste your time and get a hold of this recipe book.

The recipes in the book are easily to cook and will enable you to become an outstanding chef in a very short time. The Instant Pot will help you out in having these delicious recipes to yourself in a less time, without much effort and yet the food you will serve yourself and your loved ones will have no match to it whether it is the taste or the nutrients, it can never be more perfect.

In this sedative and busy life, this book will prove to be a turning point in making you healthy in almost every dimension of your life.

Made in the USA
San Bernardino, CA
19 December 2018